A THRICE-TOLD TALE

A THRICE-TOLD TALE

Feminism, Postmodernism, and
Ethnographic Responsibility

Margery Wolf

STANFORD UNIVERSITY PRESS
STANFORD, CALIFORNIA

Stanford University Press
Stanford, California
© 1992 by the Board of Trustees of the
Leland Stanford Junior University
Printed in the United States of America

CIP data appear at the end of the book

For Mac

Preface

My previous books were written as the products of particular field projects. This book came out of a casual conversation with Carol A. Smith and Muriel Bell while driving in the highlands of Guatemala. That conversation led me to set aside the somewhat pedestrian book I had been given a semester's leave to complete and to pursue an idea. I learned much more than I had expected as a result of that pursuit—about my own perspective on ethnography as well as about that of others.

Discussions of the postmodernist critiques of ethnography and the feminist critiques of anthropology and postmodernism always seem a bit testy. I don't want to add to that tone, but I have stated my opinions and biases frankly. Whether or not readers agree with my thoughts on some of these debates, I hope they will find the three texts around which they are organized useful pedagogical tools.

I have been blessed with good friends and kind readers who have pointed out where I had gone too far and yet encouraged me to go a little further. I am grateful to Florence Babb, who critiqued a shaky first draft; David Arkush, who as a historian with philosophical tendencies gave me an invaluable reading; Robert J. Smith, who read the manuscript with the sharp eye of a good critic and the charitable words of an old and dear friend; Kathleen Newman, who examined the manuscript from the perspective of a different breed of postmodernist and gave me invaluable advice that, had I incorporated it all, would have doubled the size of the book; and Annette Weiner, my "anonymous" reviewer, who provided both encouraging words and excellent suggestions. My gratitude to them all. And finally, my thanks to Mac Marshall, who took on more than his share of our domestic chores, read bits and pieces, drafts and revised drafts, and reminded me at just the right time whom the book was for: anthropologists and their students, who may also be wondering if there really is a crisis in ethnography and if ethnography will survive it. If I have learned nothing else in writing this book, it is that ethnography remains and will remain for many years to come a vibrant source of information about the wondrous diversity of human experiences.

M.W.

Contents

A THRICE-TOLD TALE

CHAPTER ONE

Ruminations with a View(point)

THIS IS NOT a book for postmodernists, nor is it a book for their critics.* This is a book for anthropologists and other social scientists who, like me, have read and listened with interest to the protagonists' often heated exchanges—over polyvocality, reflexivity, colonialist discourse, audience, the nature of the relationship between anthropologist and informants, and the like—and still are just a little more interested in the content of the ethnographies we read and write than in the ethnographers' epistemologies. I do not intend by this comment to suggest disdain for the work of postmodernists like James Clifford, Michael M. J. Fischer, George E. Marcus, and Stephen Tyler. On the contrary, I find their analyses of ethnographic frailties and failings useful on the whole, and I think that their criticisms of ethnographers and their habits cannot but improve the product of those who give their arguments a fair reading. But, like most anthropologists, I remain more interested in why Chinese peasants do what they do, and, as Graham Watson (1987: 36) puts it, in "getting the news out." I see much in the postmodernist ruminations that helps me toward that goal but much also that does not seem to me in the best interests of anthropology at all.

*I recognize that postmodernists are as diverse as feminists in their positions on many of the issues I will be raising here. I use the labels in similar ways, the one to identify academics who are currently more preoccupied with the way ethnography is written than with the way research is carried out, and the other to identify scholars who seek to understand and dismantle gender hierarchies in their intellectual as well as personal worlds.

This is also a book for feminist social scientists who have long been concerned about some of the issues only now troubling (some) ethnographers, such as whether by studying our subjects we are also exploiting them and whether by attempting to improve women's living situations we are imposing another (powerful) society's values. What may at first seem an ethical intervention in terms of feminist principles, for example, can seem decidedly less ethical when one observes the effect of a particular change on other actors in the drama of village life. Who is to decide?

Although feminist theory has been ignored by the new critics of ethnography (a topic I will return to in more detail below), postmodernism is having a powerful influence on some feminists and a growing influence on feminist social scientists. To my thinking, there are some good things coming out of this intellectual encounter, but again, as with anthropology and postmodernism there are some dangers, both theoretically and politically.

This book is a personal exploration of some of these issues. It came about because, a few years ago, I discovered in my files a short story I had written nearly thirty years ago while living in a small village in northern Taiwan. I had forgotten writing the story, but after a search through fieldnotes and a reading of my journals for that period, the events that precipitated the story began to come back in almost unwelcome detail—sounds, smells, visual images, and emotional states. But what surprised me as I read and reread the various written records was that the fieldnotes, the journals, and the short story represented quite different versions of what had happened.

Moreover, as I thought about what had occurred, I realized that I was thinking about those long-ago events in a very different way than I did when they were dutifully recorded in my notes and, less dutifully, in the story. At that time, I thought of myself as the wife and assistant of an anthropologist who was on his first field trip; now, I think of myself as an anthropologist. At that time, they were notes on one more exciting event in the exotic environment in which I found myself living; now, they are an intriguing record of the ideology and social context that led residents of a small village to reach one conclusion about a member of their community rather than another. They have become data, interesting data that should be analyzed and shared with my intellectual community in the usual academic format, a book or a journal article, rather than in the fictionalized format I had used so many years earlier.

This could have been a simple project, but as I reviewed the old fieldnotes and mused over the short story that contradicted both some of the "facts" and some of the anthropological attitudes recorded there, I was also catching up on my general reading. I found myself enmeshed in the debates set off by the collection of articles edited by James Clifford and George Marcus (*Writing Culture*, 1986) and in the postmodernist critiques of ethnography generally, and the feminist critiques of postmodernism specifically.

Reflexivity was not a topic of much interest when Arthur Wolf and I first did field research in the late 1950s and early 1960s. We struggled to understand the cultures we studied, to be ethical in our interactions with our informants, and to stay out of trouble with the ruling party. When we analyzed our data and wrote them up, we felt a responsibility to "our" village to "get it right," but they were "our" data, not theirs, and we assumed only our reputations as scholars would be affected by not "getting it right." Our academic mentors stressed objectivity and minimal disruption of our informants' daily lives. Those of us who were on our first field trips were usually trying to live on a shoestring and, in Taiwan, at least, were often treated by our hosts with a slightly patronizing indulgence of our "barbarian ignorance." We would have had to think a while before we could recognize the enormity of the power differential between us and, for example, the domineering, nagging, and much beloved cook we hired. When we finally sat down to write up our data, being experimental with form or analysis was not encouraged. If we wanted to be taken seriously as scholars and to have our interpretation of Society X accepted, we knew that there was a style of presentation within which we had to work.

So, some thirty years later, when I turned to reconstruct certain events that occurred in the early spring of 1960 in the little village of Peihotien, I approached the fieldnotes and my personal journals not only as a very different person (a feminist anthropologist) but also in a very different anthropological climate, one in which the discipline is being buffeted by criticism from without and from within about the value, indeed, the very integrity of its product, the ethnography. Where once I was satisfied to describe what I thought I saw and heard as accurately as possible, to the point of trying to resolve differences of opinion among my informants, I have come to realize the importance of retaining these "contested meanings." But only to a point, and that point is where my path diverges from that of the postmodernist critics of ethnography.

My view of China does not, by a long shot, reflect the views of all the people with whom I have talked. My ethnographic work represents my understanding of China as a result of conversations held and conversations overheard. Some of these conversations were foolish and ill-informed, and a few were designed to mislead; other conversations were with or between people who had only a superficial understanding of a topic—no matter how deep their understanding of other areas of life might be. (Sometime ask your Uncle Ned who works for Acme Hardware and knows all there is to know about wrenches what consciousness raising is.) Even the most ardent critic of old-fashioned ethnography would surely grant an authorial license to edit some of these flawed perspectives, but there are other differences in local understandings that perhaps ought not to have been resolved. Like most scholars who happen to reread some of their early work (not recommended), there are some things I wish I could revise, but in general, I still see my ethnographic responsibility as including an effort to make sense out of what I saw, was told, or read—first for myself and then for my readers.

Some postmodern critics question the very possibility of ethnographers representing the experience of another culture, and others question the ethics of even attempting to do so, seeing the process itself as an exercise in colonialism (domination). The questioning is important, the answers less so. Obviously (or so it seems to me), anthropologists can only convey their own understandings of their observations in another culture in their ethnographies. The better the observer, the more likely she is to catch her informants' understanding of the meaning of their experiences; the better the writer, the more likely she is to be able to convey that meaning to an interested reader from another culture. Some kinds of cultural meanings *may* only be accurately understood and reported by one who has learned them without realizing it, but much of the cultural onion may be as easily or even more easily picked apart by a careful analyst who is not of the culture.* It would be as great a loss to have first-world anthropologists confine their research to the first world as it is (currently) to have third-world anthropologists confine theirs to the third world.

Edward Said (1978) and those who accept his "orientalism" critique assert that ethnographic research is but another form of white domination, an ethical concern that is shared by many anthropologists. Labeling fieldwork an act of colonialism is an obvious overstatement, designed to draw our attention to the ways in which white privilege affects anthropological fieldwork. Certainly, we have plenty of historical evidence of careful, sensitive ethnographies being used by co-

---

*David Arkush pointed out to me that the best literary translations are those in which one is translating *into* one's native language. Although applying this to the interpretation of culture is appealing as a metaphor, it is difficult to support empirically for the obvious reason that cultural interpretation is imprecise and open to equally valid alternative readings.

lonial regimes to tighten their control over "the natives." That kind of obvious cultural domination is less common now, but the subtler kinds of domination—the sort that women have experienced in their own cultures and recognize with dismay in their research and that of their male colleagues— still haunts us. Power differentials within this society and between us and those we study exist and, alas, will continue to exist for the foreseeable future. Anthropologists must be constantly aware of how these differences in power can distort their perceptions and skew their interpretations. Obviously, they must also be careful not to take advantage of their (usually) considerably greater power in ways that will disadvantage the people they are studying.

But these dangers should not require abandoning crossnational research. Such a renunciation hardly seems ethical when one considers how often authoritarian regimes control information coming in and going out, information about living conditions, for example, that might be relevant to the survival of some groups and some ideas. There is a curious postmodernist politics that condemns us for our individual colonialist attitudes but remains aloof from the often bloody results of oppressive governments, of the left and the right. Feminist anthropologists, on the other hand, often find themselves caught between their own commitment to improving the lives of women everywhere and their discipline's concern about interference in local politics. The power that accrues to being first world in a third-world country cannot be denied and yet cannot be used without alienating somebody. Postmodernism gives us little guidance here.

For anthropologists, Clifford and Marcus have become the symbols of the postmodernist critique of ethnography, and their *Writing Culture* the focal text—although there are a good many others who line up on the postmodernist side of the barricades. On both sides of the debate, as well as in the spectators' gallery, one can find feminist social scientists who are indignant and at the same time wryly amused to hear the critiques they have leveled for years now being translated into postmodernist terminology and taken *very* seriously. If there is any page James Clifford has written that he may wish he hadn't, I suspect it is the section in his Introduction to *Writing Culture* where he lamely explains the absence of a feminist paper in the collection. Clifford in particular and postmodernists in general have been roundly criticized for their male bias (e.g., Caplan 1989: 15; Gordon 1988: 14–15; Mascia-Lees et al. 1989: 11). I have a few things to add to this criticism, but I will also take issue in the pages and chapters that follow with some of the feminist positions on doing ethnography.

Before I get further into these issues, let me explain what follows. Because I did analyze and publish the material that led to the writing of the short story mentioned above (Wolf 1990a), I now have three texts describing in different ways what happened in the little village of Peihotien some thirty years ago. One is a piece of fiction written by me alone; another consists of unanalyzed fieldnotes recording interviews and observations collected by any of the several members of the field staff; and the third is entirely in my voice, written in a style acceptable to referees chosen by the *American Ethnologist*. Each text takes a different perspective, is written in a different style, and has different "outcomes," yet all three involve the same set of events. Not surprisingly, in each can be found examples of the attitudes, methods, and ideas that our postmodern critics both hate and love. The three texts are presented here as Chapters Two, Three, and Four with minimal editorial interventions. Each chapter is followed by a Commentary, in which I use the text to illustrate and argue with some of the problems and promises this new period of reflexivity has brought to the fore.

Because in the rest of this chapter I want to draw on the ethnographic material that forms the backbone of this book, I must risk creating here a fourth version of what occurred in Peihotien in 1960. A young mother of three children began to behave in a decidedly aberrant, perhaps suicidal, manner. Over a period of about a month, she displayed symptoms of mental illness, spirit loss, possession by a god, and shamanism. Anyone who has lived in a small village will understand that this behavior would not long go unnoticed by her neighbors and would quickly become the major topic of conversation whenever two people met. Eventually, people from nearby communities became involved, and at times there were literally crowds surrounding her house and filling her courtyard. Mrs. Tan was an "outsider" as far as the local people were concerned, because she and her family had only lived in the village for ten years; to be a "real" member of the community, one had to be associated with a family that had been there at least a generation, preferably two.

Following Mrs. Tan's first public outburst, she was quickly hustled off to a "hospital" in the nearby market town, where she was kept under physical restraints (tied to a bed) and psychological restraints (drugged). After a few days, she returned to the village, and before she was finally taken away from the area to her mother's house, she was considered by some members of the community to be a *tang-ki*, or shaman, through whom a god was speaking.* Throughout this period, the villagers debated among themselves and with ritual specialists—often in her presence—about whether she was "crazy," had simply lost her soul (a fairly common occurrence), had been chosen as a vehicle for a god who wished direct access to believers (a recognized status), or was being exploited by her ne'er-do-well husband, who thought he could make money off her role as a *tang-ki*. I suspect for some villagers this debate was never truly resolved; for others, it was settled when she left the village with her mother.

This is a simple story that could have been told (and undoubtedly has been) by many, many people. To my knowledge, only mine has been written, let alone published, freezing

---

*I use shamanism and spirit possession interchangeably and refer to the practitioners as shamans, spirit mediums, or *tang-ki*, as they are called in Taiwan.

it unnaturally and giving it unearned legitimacy. In Chapter Three, the events appear as a jumble of field observations and interviews. Arguably, this record could be considered the voice of the anthropologist. However, as I point out in the introductory paragraphs to that chapter, our field assistant, Wu Chieh, a young Taiwanese woman with the equivalent of a tenth-grade education, did the majority of the observing and interviewing, and in a very real sense defined the topic.* She had been working with us for nearly two years, and she had learned to formulate questions and report answers in a format that was comfortable to our Western minds. She had come to look for, or at least to recognize, the kinds of issues that interested us. Even so, I felt then and continue to feel that the interest she took in these events was not as our employee but as one of Mrs. Tan's neighbors. She also had a sympathy for Mrs. Tan as a fellow outsider that many of our neighbors did not and could not share. She pursued the story and people's reactions to the obviously exciting activities that it encompassed with a personal concern that she rarely exercised in her other work with us. Nonetheless, the fieldnotes are a mélange of voices that were selected for recording from the yet more numerous set of voices still echoing in our ears when we sat down at the end of each day to write up the day's notes.

In Chapter Four, the voice is clearly that of the anthropologist telling the story in the context of shamanism in Taiwan. I wanted to explore the factors in the community's final decision about the nature of Mrs. Tan's behavior. I made use of the voices that Wu Chieh provided in her interviews and observations, but my interpretations of them were based on my

*This is, as with all names in this book, a fictitious name. The choice of romanizations may seem bizarre in the texts. For Taiwanese, I use Bodman (1955), and for Mandarin Chinese, I use a modified Wade-Giles because the texts are from Taiwan where the romanization sponsored by the People's Republic of China was not (and is not) used. Most, but not all, Taiwanese names and words are given in that language, but those who interacted with us primarily in Mandarin were given Mandarin rather than Taiwanese names because that is the way they presented themselves to us (e.g. Wu Chieh).

understanding of where those voices were coming from in relation to their status, Mrs. Tan's status, and the cultural context. My control over possibly competing interpretations is determined by my ability to comprehend and process the data available.

Chapter Two, the short story called "The Hot Spell," might conceivably be labeled "experimental ethnography," but it was written as fiction—not as fact using fictional forms, as some postmodernists urge. The "I" voice, and I admit it still does feel a bit like me, is totally in control of the information. The action and emotions are presented directly, and even the doubts and conflicted voices come from the author, no matter how carefully worded between the quotation marks. A few, but very few, of the lines quoted appear somewhere in the fieldnotes or in my journals, although even now, many years since I have spoken or even heard that dialect, I can hear cadences and recognize the individuals who were amalgamated into a single character.

Had I time enough while in the field—and my readers patience enough—these events could have been recounted in numerous other voices. Many actors and observers could have been given the space for their accounts, their interpretations, of what happened in March 1960. Perhaps the most interesting would have been Mrs. Tan's interpretation, which I suspect would have changed from day to day. Another fascinating perspective would have been that of the coterie of old women who controlled so much more of village opinion than anyone, including the middle-aged men who often "voiced" village opinion, realized. Wu Chieh's own full account (there was much she did not tell me even off the record) might be very different from any of those presented here. The village children—who after any major event (such as New Year's or a god's birthday celebration) spent days incorporating vivid, and often embarrassing, imitations of adult behavior into their play—could have provided another sharp set of insights. And, of course, the ritual specialists—the *tang-ki* who tried to lure back Mrs. Tan's wandering soul, and the old man I call Ong Hue-lieng, who made the final pronouncement about her possession—both would have had very different accounts to present.

All of these speakers, including those presented fully in the pages that follow, interpret events with a vested interest, some consciously and some in total innocence. My failure to involve all these interpretations in this account was perhaps a failure in fieldwork (although these events *were* peripheral to what we were studying), but have I robbed my informants of their authority as the holders of their culture or, perhaps worse, assigned that authority to some rather than others? I think not. Their authority is intact: I do not speak for them but about them, even though I occasionally use their voices to tell my story.

The anthropologist listens to as many voices as she can and then chooses among them when she passes their opinions on to members of another culture. The choice is not arbitrary, but then neither is the testimony. However, no matter what format the anthropologist/reporter/writer uses, she eventually takes the responsibility for putting down the words, for converting their possibly fleeting opinions into a text. I see no way to avoid this exercise of power and at least some of the stylistic requirements used to legitimate that text if the practice of ethnography is to continue.

I am aware that to some this position is blasphemous, to others obvious, and to still others lacking in sophistication (Sangren 1988: 406). I am also aware that it questions principles feminists have been attempting to formulate concerning nonexploitative research methods. These problems will be further explored in the commentaries and the final chapter.

So much has been written about the self/other, subject/object dilemmas that I would prefer to keep my distance from what seems to be in some instances a philosophical problem, in others a literary one, and nearly always a political one. The Other is a perfect concept for postmodernists because it is constantly having to be redefined, is nearly always vague in its boundaries, and is as luxuriant in meanings as it is constrained by specificity. For Marilyn Strathern (1987), the feminists' Other is men/patriarchy, and something to be attacked, whereas the anthropologists' Other is the culture under study and something "to create a relation with" (289), to preserve, and/or interpret, a situation she finds "awkward," at least for feminist anthropologists. Pat Caplan (1988) points out that feminist anthropologists have a lot more Others to contend with than Strathern recognizes, a position with which I heartily agree. In the three texts presented here, separating Subject from Other is not so simple as one might expect, even though acts and actors are much the same in each. At times, the Subject becomes the Other and neither is Me.

Whether or not an anthropologist believes she creates, interprets, or describes culture, she must recognize that she creates "Others" as the result of her work, and that she must bear some responsibility for those Others. Since for many feminists this idea reminds us of our own construction as man's "Other," that which varies from the male norm, we are uneasy. Anthropologists are particularly vulnerable to charges that we assume our superiority over those we study because we typically study the rural, the poor, and the uneducated and, according to Chandra Mohanty (1984: 337), cast them as deviations from a white, educated, middle-class norm:

Without the overdetermined discourse that creates the *third* world, there would be no (singular and privileged) first world. Without the "third world woman," the particular self-presentation of Western women mentioned above [secular, liberated, and with control over their own lives] would be problematical. *I am suggesting then that the one enables and sustains the other.* (Mohanty 1984: 353; italics mine)

Mohanty, however, falls into the same trap by characterizing first-world feminist anthropology in terms of the writings of a few anthropologists who have published with the very specialized Zed Press.

On the whole, I accept the accusations of colonialism, ethnocentrism, racism, and imperialism that we have grappled with in recent decades, but, without cutting off debate, I hope we can now also get on with the work of creating a more equitable world. Mohanty concludes her essay with this sage observation: "It is time to move beyond the Marx who found it possible to say: They cannot represent themselves; they must be represented" (1984: 354). And it is reassuring to see that more and more of the "underrepresented" are now doing the work necessary to "represent themselves" (and, I might add, encountering some of the same resentment and accusations of elitism that white first-world anthropologists have experienced). We as anthropologists can only try to be sensitive to the implications of our perceived status, implications that may be even more troubling for the fieldworker who works in her own society. As Susan Bordo wisely counsels:

It is impossible to be "politically correct." For the dynamics of inclusion and exclusion . . . are played out on multiple and shifting fronts, and all ideas (no matter how "liberatory" in some contexts or for some purposes) are condemned to be haunted by a voice from the margins already speaking (or perhaps presently muted but awaiting the conditions for speech), awakening us to what has been excluded, effaced, damaged. (1990: 138)

No matter how careful, I fear all of us who do research must be prepared to be the resented Other to the "objects" of our study.

The manner in which that resentment is expressed varies across cultures, within cultures, and even within villages, but it usually involves a desire for a redistribution of wealth. Intellectuals of the culture with which we are engaged are most likely to accuse us of misappropriating power, of using powerless women in Taiwan, India, or Africa to make careers for ourselves. They ask what we give in exchange, and we are hard put to give them answers, or at least answers that do not sound defensive or self-serving. Nonetheless, I do not think we need to hang our heads in shame. I do not apologize for the research I have done or the books I have written about Taiwanese women. When I began my research, there were no Taiwanese scholars who were the least bit interested in women's lives. I may not have always gotten it right, but Taiwanese *women* were taken seriously as agents because of my research and writing. Now they can speak for themselves or through the work of a group of young Taiwanese feminist scholars. But note that these new scholars will also speak of a vastly changed society. The question Bordo puts to critics of a similar historical development in feminist theory is equally applicable here: "Could we now speak of the differences that inflect *gender* if gender had not first been shown to make a difference?" (1990: 141)

Enough ruminating for now. Let us return to a less complex time and a less complex view of it. I present the short story as the first text in this nontextual analysis because I think (and some friends who have read the chapter in draft agree) that it gives readers who have never been to a Taiwanese village, let alone lived in one, a sense of village life that they cannot get from the fieldnotes or the article. There are other reasons for the order of the chapters—the degree to which they illustrate differences in ethnographic authority, for one—that I hope will be clear as the reader progresses.

CHAPTER TWO

The Hot Spell

TYPHOON WARNINGS had been out for two weeks, but each storm passed us by, either twisting over to ease Hong Kong's water shortage or moving west into the open Pacific. The thick, heavy air over northern Taiwan hung motionless, absorbing heat and pressing it down on our heads. My husband, an anthropologist, and I had been living for over a year with a Taiwanese farm family in a small village an hour away from the city of Taipei. Most of the summer the thick brick walls and heavy tile roof protected us from the semitropical sun that penetrated the flimsy houses of city-dwellers. In the evenings, at least the suggestion of a breeze usually moved across the flooded paddies, creating cool whispers in the growing rice and clearing the house of the day's collection of heat. But for two weeks now, there had been no whispering in the rice paddies, no relief with darkness from the oppressive heat. My lethargy turned to depression and then to sodden tension.

At first I thought it self-generated, but as I wandered through the village, halfheartedly interviewing mothers about toilet training, I saw the same dull tension on other faces. Only an ancient lady with tiny bound feet greeted me as usual. Eighty-five years of exposure to alternations of heat and humidity and cold and humidity had brought her invulnerability. So-cu sipped hot water (the tea of the poor) and warned me, "Someone has angered Tien Kung. He is sending his little typhoons away. He will send us a bad one soon." She droned on for an hour with stories of the capriciousness of gods, of natural disasters sent by the gods in days gone by, of the human frailties that caused them. An hour of excellent data from an anthropologist's perspective. I took notes on my limp tablet and hoped that Wu Chieh, my field assistant, was tucking away some of the linguistic subtleties that were still beyond me. We returned to the house, stopping briefly in the courtyard to commiserate with Lim Ge-gou, the wife of our host, as she looked at her dwindling flock of baby chicks. Each day two or three more drooped and died. Four were left, pecking listlessly at grains of rice. Mrs. Lim's face also was a mixture of strain and apathy.

Inside, the house was dim but no cooler. Smells that ordinarily suggested themselves and disappeared seemed solid in the heavy air. The smell from the privy dominated the back rooms; the pungent decaying smell of preserved vegetables clung to the air in the kitchen and inner courtyard; in the guest hall, generations of incense burned on the ancestral altar hung black and heavy; the dusty yellow odor of a year's cigarette smoke greeted me at the door of the room we used as an office. I tried to remember the smell of the mint growing in the backyard of my mother's home in northern California.

After lunch, my husband left for a few days in Taipei to search out some land records, Wu Chieh departed with her stopwatch to do child observations, and I settled in the office, collating data and typing up back fieldnotes. The heat intensified as the hour hand moved downward, silencing the five hundred people who lived in the village. The only sound was the rustle of paper as I shifted to another chart—not even the complaining wail of an infant, an invariant of village life, moved the air. A dull throb set up in the back of my head. I leaned back in my chair, pulling at my damp shirt, and wondered vaguely if we had any aspirin left.

I may have been sitting there for a minute or an hour when I heard a sound that lowered my body temperature by ten degrees and pulled the hair of my scalp into a knot. It started with a low bovine moan and undulated up the scale into an intense piercing scream. At its peak, it dropped off into almost a gargle, stopped briefly, and then on a lower scale was punctuated by a series of short hoarse shrieks. For a few seconds there was silence. Then sounds came from everywhere— wooden clogs rushing along packed earth paths, doors banging, questioning voices edged with fear. Even with my limited knowledge of Hokkien, I could comprehend the questions being shouted: "What is it? Who? What's happened?" I hurried through the house to the back door, nearly colliding with other family members heading in the same direction.

The path, usually empty at this time of day, seemed filled with people. A few were rushing along with their eyes fixed on something in the distance, others were clumping uncertainly, eyes fixed on those who seemed to have a goal—all were asking, "What is it?" I looked down the path toward where the village ends and the rice paddy begins and saw a small crowd looking into the paddy and gesturing excitedly. I joined them, but no one had time for me and my clumsily worded questions. People were pushing for position on the edge of the rice paddy and talking excitedly about what they were observing.

Taking advantage of my height and a conveniently forgotten bamboo stool, I looked over their heads at the source of the inhuman high-pitched groans that continued to issue from the paddy. Mr. Tan, an unemployed laborer, and two of his neighbors, both middle-aged women, were trying to drag a struggling, slime-covered woman out of the muck of the paddy. Just after I reached my observation post, she gave up her battle with a low despairing moan. As they pulled her onto the path above the paddy, I recognized her as Mr. Tan's wife, a shy reserved woman in her early thirties, the mother of three children. The crowd divided, part of them following Mr. Tan and one of the women carrying Mrs. Tan, the other half encircling the second woman with questions. Wu Chieh was standing near the door of the Tans' house. Clinging to her skirt, looking very pale and frightened, were the two older Tan children. She turned and led them into the house. Mrs. Kho, one of the women in the paddy, was trying to answer the excited questions swirling around her. I picked out a few sentences, but none of them seemed to link together in an explanation I could comprehend. The pressure of my inadequacies and of the relentless sun drove me back to the Lim house.

Once or twice during the afternoon I heard a bicycle picking its way up the path toward the market town. Later, an empty pedicab rattled into the village. Shortly after, it left again, slower and clearly occupied. The mountains that rim the Taipei basin began to recede and finally to blur as the heat and humidity of late afternoon bore steadily down. The village no longer seemed empty, but all sounds seemed muffled, as though people were moving about cautiously. The occasional wail of a miserable infant was quickly silenced. From my window I could see a group of children who at this time of day usually sneaked off to wade or paddle in the forbidden river behind the village. They sat under the big tree that shades the Tu Ti Kung shrine, rolling a few marbles around and talking softly. I heard the slip-slop, slip-slop of Wu Chieh's *zori* as she walked across the cement floor toward the office. Her young face looked strained. She sat down, tense and tired.

'Ah, that Tan Tien-lai. He is so stupid. You know his nickname is Dumb Tien-lai . . . For two days Mrs. Tan has been beating at her chest saying it was on fire and doing strange things. He just squats there looking at her and saying, 'She is going crazy again.' Yesterday, she took the baby over to her sister in San Chung Pu and asked her to take care of her for a while. She knew this was going to happen, but Dumb Tien-lai, he just squats there and stares at her."

"How is she now?"

"Mrs. Li made him go get the doctor, and she and Mrs. Kho washed her off, just like a baby. She lay there just like a baby . . . But she kept begging them for a stick of incense, just one stick of incense. They finally gave her one and she lay there with it in her hands, mumbling strange words. When her husband and the doctor came, she jumped up and tried to run again, but they caught her and the doctor gave her a shot that put her to sleep. Then they took her off to the little hospital."

"Little hospital?"

"Well, they call it a hospital, but it is just an old store in Tapu near the doctor's house. It has a couple of beds in it and an old lady to take care of it."

"What else?"

Wu Chieh was having trouble meeting my eyes. There was a squirminess in her manner that I had seen before when a subject of our research touched on a belief or a custom she wished to avoid, either from delicacy or from personal uncertainty. To give her time, I launched into a brief lecture on the nature of mental illness and its relationship to other illnesses. She politely ignored me and peeled an orange.

"Some say she isn't crazy. Maybe its something else . . ."

"Something else?"

"Mmmm."

"What else? What do you mean?"

"I don't know." When Wu Chieh uses the phrase "I don't know," she uses it as a direct translation from the Mandarin *pu hsiao te*. Sometimes she doesn't even bother to translate it into English. What it means is either "I know nothing about this subject and I don't care to learn anything about it," or "There is nothing more I wish to say about the subject." When she says it, in Chinese or English, I know I have reached the end of that particular path.

"How did she get into the rice paddy?"

"She jumped in."

"Ugh."

"Well, she made a mistake. She was trying to get to the river."

"Oh." A river is a traditional site for suicides or suicide

attempts, particularly among Taiwanese women. Wu Chieh understood the significance of my "oh."

"She wasn't trying to do that. She . . ." Her eyes dropped again. I tried to find another question that couldn't be answered with *pu hsiao te*.

"How do you know she wasn't trying to do that?"

"She said so. She said she had to go there to meet someone, something . . ." To my amazement, Wu Chieh burst into tears and rushed out of the room. I felt two rivulets of sweat join between my shoulder blades and trickle down my backbone. I had no desire to torment the girl further; I wished the real anthropologist would come home and free me of obligation. I was too hot and miserable to be curious, but I turned to the fieldnotes to see what other information we had about the Tan family.

Mr. Tan, an affable, feckless young man, brought his wife and newborn son to Peihotien about eight years ago. They rented part of a ramshackle old farmhouse. He worked for a while as a laborer in the winery in Tapu, lost that job, and then moved to another in the area. His police registration included his younger sister as part of their family. She visited them every three or four months but was employed in Taipei, ostensibly as a clerk, but more likely as a bar girl. He had no other living siblings, and both of his parents were dead. His neighbors considered him good-natured, dull-witted, and temporary. The label "temporary" is attached to the handful of families who rent houses or parts of houses in the village; "newcomers" is reserved for those families who have owned land in the area for only two or three generations; the "old" families of the village, three-fourths of whom are related, have no need to count generations of residence, even though they may no longer own any more land than what they live on, if that.

Mrs. Tan was considered by her neighbors to be a shy, quiet woman who kept to herself. She followed the typical Taiwanese pattern of having a child every two years, but each birth was difficult and left her ill for several weeks. Since she had no relatives nearby, one of the neighbor women usually assisted her out of kindness. Her agony in childbirth was a source of scorn for some of the hardy younger women, proud of their ability to give birth stoically. Mrs. Tan was unusually fond of her children, particularly the girl. Her only trouble with her neighbors was over children's quarrels—she was fiercely protective of her own. She and her children, as "temporary" residents, usually got the worst of it. According to my fieldnotes, our Wu Chieh was an unwilling witness to the incident that caused her to sever relations with the large Lim family who lived nearby. One day, after the disputed outcome of a game, the Lim children ganged up on Mrs. Tan's eldest boy, tore his clothing, and bloodied his nose. When she went to discuss the matter with the Lims, one of the daughters-in-law of the family turned her away curtly. "If children fight and kill each other, it serves them right. If your children get killed, then you come and take them home and bury them. You don't need to come and tell me about it." Mrs. Tan was hurt and angry. Her children were under strict orders from then on to avoid the Lim children—which they did when she was present and didn't when she wasn't.

Mrs. Tan chose most of her friends from the older women who lived nearby. They appreciated her attention and were impressed with her piety. Because of her husband's inability to hold a steady job, providing food for her children was a daily struggle, but she never neglected sacrifices to his ancestors or any of the special sacrifices required on the birthdays of the gods of the area. She often went to the local temples for advice from the gods and attended many sessions given by local and visiting shamans to seek cures for her children's illnesses or relief from her husband's bad fortune. These shamans are men or (rarely) women whose bodies are temporarily possessed by one of the gods. While the god is in residence in the shaman's body, he or (even more rarely) she can be approached by supplicants for advice on personal matters, business matters, and illnesses. Speaking through the shaman, the god answers questions in a god's voice—very unlike the shaman's natural voice—or writes out advice and opinions in an unusual, but readable script.

Some of the *tang-ki*, as they are called locally, are out-and-out fakes, whose shows of spirit possession with accompanying tremors and twitchings have become routine and apparently effortless performances. Others endure the convulsions of what seem to be epileptic seizures and are very sincere in their dealings with supplicants. The former make a good income; the latter often die young. The predictions of both are valued. Their audience includes women and men of all ages. Farmers come for information about sick pigs; mothers seek advice on controlling wayward sons; sons come for medicine to cure the illnesses of elderly parents; young women come for cures for infertility. According to our records, Mrs. Tan asked the god to help find employment for her husband on one occasion and a cure for her son's boils on another.

I listlessly flipped on through the fieldnotes. Mrs. Tan's name appeared on the list we had made of the more conservative villagers who had objected to changing the date for the celebration of the god Tzu Shih Yeh's birthday to coincide with another festival, a plan that would save everyone the expense of two feasts within ten days. There was another pathetic observation that Wu Chieh had reported to us on the god Shang Ti Kung's birthday. She had spotted Mrs. Tan hanging around the back of the temple until it was nearly dark, before she placed her offering on the altar. Instead of the usual gift of five kinds of meat, she had only been able to buy two eggs and a small piece of pork fat. She told Wu Chieh she was embarrassed to have her neighbors see her meager offering and fearful that the god would be offended.

My notes had very little information about the children. They were woefully underweight, smaller than their peers, and tended to respond to assaults with tears and retreat rather than the counterattacks that would have given them a toehold in the play group. Instead of simply walking up and joining a game, the older boy asked if he could play and was often turned away—partly because excluding him gave his peers a sense of power and partly because he did not have the physical stamina to make him a desirable teammate.

I turned from the notes in disgust. The details might differ, but the general outlines of Mrs. Tan's life might describe a third of the rural women in Taiwan. There was nothing there to explain why a woman threw herself in the steaming stinking muck of a rice paddy.

Liang Chieh, cook, housekeeper, and self-appointed guardian of our health and morals, called me to dinner. My request for a glass of cold water was answered with a glass of lukewarm tea and a lecture (not the first) on the dangers of cold water in hot weather. When my husband was at home, Liang Chieh was Older Sister. When he was away, she was Mother-in-law. Before the villagers, she was willing to pretend she was our employee; an American guest was assumed, by coloring, to be our relative, her responsibility, and therefore subject to the same badgering we received. On more than one occasion, we had been grateful that her heavy Shanghai accent made her Mandarin nearly incomprehensible to strangers and totally incomprehensible to the Hokkien-speaking villagers.

It was not a particularly lively dinner. Wu Chieh brooded over her rice bowl, and even Liang Chieh could not work up her usual enthusiasm over the recitation of the prices asked for the contents of our dinner and the prices she paid after ruthless bargaining. I escaped as soon as I could to the front courtyard to watch the Lim family children squabbling half-heartedly over the gleanings from our office wastebasket. It grew darker, but not cooler. The children wandered off to fall asleep in places where their mothers could conveniently find them and put them, sleepily protesting, to bed. I stayed on, slapping hopelessly at mosquitoes. After a while, Lim Han-cu, the head of our extended family, came out, and we chatted in the peculiar combination of Hokkien and Mandarin that we had settled upon shortly after I arrived in the village. We exchanged weather reports and the state of his wife's now one remaining chick before I asked him if he had heard about Mrs. Tan's unusual paddy activities. He had, but dismissed the topic with a terse comment about superstitious women. I asked if she had ever behaved this way before, and he answered with unusual abruptness, "I don't know anything about them. They are new people." Even Mr. Lim was edgy.

Two days later, I got a note from my husband in Taipei, exultant about a cache of Japanese colonial records he had heard of and a manuscript he'd found, with a depressing last sentence that he wouldn't be back for several more days. I tuned in the Armed Forces Radio Service in time to hear a slightly nasal Midwestern voice announce happily that the typhoon I had been counting on had veered off to sea. He was no doubt broadcasting from an air-conditioned studio. Wu Chieh wandered in, looking hot and irritable.

"They won't do anything."

"Huh? Who?"

"The kids. There isn't anything to observe. They just sit and push sticks and rocks around. They don't even fight over them."

"Did you try the riverbank?"

"This is the Seventh Month. Even He-iam wouldn't go there now." (He-iam is the village bad boy.)

"Seventh Month?"

Wu Chieh looked disgusted and explained with officious patience, "I told you about the Seventh Month last week. Mr. Wolf wrote it all down. It's when the doors of Hell are opened and all the ghosts get a vacation. Nobody goes around the river in the Seventh Month because the ghosts of the people who drowned there are all free and will pull someone in to take their places. It's very dangerous this month."

I remembered. "Well, just forget the child observations for the rest of the day then. Maybe this evening if it cools off . . .

This afternoon just wander around and talk to people." I knew this would throw our observation timetable further off schedule, but there was a limit.

"Are you going to come too?"

"No."

"Shall I work on Mr. Wolf's questions?" We had a list of questions that Wu Chieh was to insert into her conversations with as many villagers as possible. They were harmless enough questions and sometimes Wu Chieh saw it as a challenging game, but other times she felt it was sneaky. I looked at my drooping research assistant and lost heart.

"Wu Chieh, why don't you just pretend to be Wu Chieh today. Take a long nap after lunch, and when you wake up, go find the coolest place in the village and sit there. If somebody comes along who wants to talk, talk. If not, fan yourself."

She looked at me curiously and then warily. "What are you going to do?"

"I am going to crawl into the icebox and close the door."

She paused to see if she had misunderstood and then left, giggling. I heard her stop to tell one of the women my weak joke. Young Mrs. Lim laughed with her, but uncertainly. She was never really sure what the foreigners her husband's uncle had introduced into the house would say or do next.

Late that afternoon, when the humidity and the heat had again formed a box around the village, I heard the homely rattle of a pedicab coming up the path from the market town. I doubt that even the rattle of a machine gun would have moved me from my chair to the window to look. A few seconds later, Wu Chieh burst into the room, energetic as a child in May, and said excitedly, "She's back. Is it safe to go see?"

I considered pretending I didn't know who "she" was, but gave it up. Mrs. Tan had returned. "Safe?"

"Well," Wu Chieh gave me her shy look, "about the mind sickness. If it's that, I don't want to catch it."

"You can't catch mental illness."

"You said it was like any other sickness, and you are always saying people can catch sickness . . ."

I had allowed another of those hopeless cultural miscommunications to form before my very eyes. "Not this sickness. You can't possibly catch what Mrs. Tan has. Nobody can."

Instead of taking the opportunity to pick away at the illogic of Western notions of medicine, one of her specialties, Wu Chieh quickly left, taking with her the sudden bright light of energy. I settled back in my chair and listened to the rustling and stirring in the village that had not been there before the rattle of the pedicab broke the sleep of late afternoon.

When Wu Chieh came back for dinner, I asked more out of a sense of duty than out of real interest how Mrs. Tan was.

"She's cold."

Forgetting, as I often did, Wu Chieh's literal English, I quipped, "Yeah, sure, so am I."

She looked at me with interest and then a small shadow of apprehension. Not being up to another discussion of contagious diseases, I quickly explained, "That was a joke."

"Oh."

"How can she possibly be cold?"

"Well, she is all huddled up, and sometimes she shivers."

"Maybe she is taking some medicine. What happened to her in the hospital?"

"They tied her to a bed and left her there."

"Surely not. Didn't she talk with someone?"

"They gave her shots two or three times a day. And Tien-lai says they charged him a lot of money. That's why he brought her home."

"You mean she is no better?"

"She is quieter . . ."

Although Wu Chieh was supposed to be out with her stopwatch doing child observations the next morning, it was clear that she spent the time at the Tan household. I was not surprised and far too uncomfortable to remonstrate with her. Besides, Wu Chieh was one of the few people in the village Mrs. Tan seemed to feel comfortable with, and Tien-lai had asked her to stay with her and the children while he went to get his mother-in-law from Keelung. I could hardly object to that. As it turned out, Tien-lai had asked her to do this the night before, but one of Wu Chieh's techniques for preserving her sense of dignity and avoiding job-endangering confrontations was to go ahead and do what she wanted and tell us about it later, should the telling become necessary. When I asked Wu Chieh what Mrs. Tan's mother was like, she seemed relieved. And that irritated me—I was not a colonial officer who expected her to be at work ten hours a day, and I hated it when she cast me in that role. For that matter, this was work—Wu Chieh was not entirely sure, even after a year of working for us, exactly where work began and "just talking" ended. I took a deep breath, reminded myself that another typhoon had been sighted, and interviewed my research assistant about her morning.

Mrs. Tan's mother was a short, square woman, neatly dressed in the subdued colors appropriate to her age. She was not well off even by Taiwanese standards, but neither was she living hand-to-mouth like her daughter. She told Wu Chieh that she had given her daughter away in adoption when she was around six years old (a not uncommon practice in the Taiwan of her childhood). The family had been well recommended, but when A-mei was thirteen or fourteen, her adoptive parents came upon a few years of hard times and sent her out to work as a servant. Something happened in the house where she was working—I suspect sexual from Wu Chieh's embarrassed look—and she wanted to return to her adoptive parents. They couldn't or wouldn't allow it; the girl became withdrawn and then exhibited behavior similar to what we were seeing in the village. She was eventually returned to her natal family. A-mei's mother insisted that this was the only other time her daughter had been "strange." She had no idea what had set her daughter off this time, but she told Wu Chieh that she intended to find out.

"She said over and over again that the last time there was no god involved . . . Uh . . . That she wanted to burn incense . . . or anything . . ." In her enthusiastic recounting of the morning's events, Wu Chieh had said more than she intended. My ears pricked up as I suddenly recalled how upset she had been when I suggested that Tan A-mei was trying to commit suicide. Something about meeting someone or something.

"And how is a god involved this time?"

Wu Chieh recovers quickly, and she was back on her feet.

"You know, she keeps wanting incense, wanting to *bai-bai* [worship by burning sticks of incense and bowing]. I *told* you."

"I don't think you told me quite all of it yet."

"Well, one of the things A-mei's mother is going to find out about is the money." She paused dramatically, hoping to deflect me with this offering. I smiled, hating myself for playing this stupid psychological game.

"Before all this happened . . . I mean before A-mei fell into the rice paddy and all . . . ninety dollars disappeared [Taiwanese currency: about three and a half days' wages for a laborer]. A-mei asked Tien-lai if he had it, and he claimed to know nothing about it. She got more and more upset, thinking she had lost it or that someone had stolen it. A-cin told me . . ."

"Wait. Who is A-cin?"

"Tan A-mei's son. He is eight or nine. Anyway, he said he saw his father take it out of her jacket pocket when he was on his way out to gamble one night. But Tien-lai, even now when she is so . . . sick, still claims that he never took it and that either she lost it or someone stole it. He is really too dumb."

"So you think he lost it gambling and is trying to make her believe she lost it?"

"That's what most people think."

"Do most people think that is why she jumped in the paddy?"

Wu Chieh looked stricken. One of her rules is that she cannot out and out lie when asked a direct question about something she doesn't want to discuss with the foreign anthropologists. "Yes" was clearly not the answer; "no" would require going even further; and by saying what "most people" thought about one intimate fact in the unfolding drama, she had lost the option of saying she didn't know what most people thought. I felt mean, but the story had now become considerably more interesting than the game of extracting it.

"Well?"

"Some do; some don't."

"Do you want to tell me about those who don't?"

"There really isn't anything to tell. Some people just don't think she's crazy."

"Come on, Wu Chieh, what *do* they think?"

"It's hard to explain."

"Try."

"Well, they think a god is calling her."

"Calling her for what? Do you mean a god wants her to kill herself?"

"No. Why do you always think that? She wasn't trying to commit suicide that day. The god was calling her and she just got confused . . ."

"Well, I am confused too. Why is a god calling Mrs. Tan?"

"Nobody knows that. They just choose some people."

"Choose them for what?"

"To speak for them . . . you know, to be their *tang-ki*."

A very inappropriate shiver went up my spine as the sweat continued to roll down it, and I was overwhelmed with a feeling of being very, very far from home—a feeling that had come less and less frequently in recent months. But as I listened to Wu Chieh, who had been my daily companion, fellow researcher, English student, and employee for fully a year, speaking about gods calling people to be *tang-ki* as if it were a not uncommon experience, I realized once again that we were separated by more than age, education, and status.

"You think this is stupid." Stupid is Wu Chieh's generic term for anything from food to local traditions that fall short of some sort of cross-cultural standard she has. In this case, I suspected that she was harking back to the lectures she used to get from her previous employer, a missionary, about foolish superstition. The Reverend Barnes had had a profound impact on Wu Chieh's life, hiring her at the age of thirteen to be an *amah* for his children after he had unintentionally run her down with his bicycle. At the time, she was selling a Chinese version of fast food from a makeshift stand on the street. Considering the poverty of her widowed mother, it is not at all clear what she might have sold next had it not been for Reverend Barnes. She quickly learned baby-talk English, and Reverend and Mrs. Barnes saw to it that she got a basic education, along with a strong dose of Christian doctrine. The latter seemed to have been only partially accepted, for when she recognized that my husband and I *really* weren't Christians, it dropped out of her conversation and practice. Out of delicacy and a rather selfish desire not to get involved with whatever soul-searching she was doing, I had not explored what her current beliefs were. But from her reaction to this conversation, I had obviously assumed a more sophisticated distance from village religion than existed.

"I haven't heard anything stupid or not stupid yet. I just want to know what people are saying about Mrs. Tan."

Enormous tears began to roll down Wu Chieh's face, and she swept them away angrily with her fists, like a small child. "I know you Americans think these are just silly superstitions . . . I think so too . . . but I *know* A-mei. When the god comes . . . it's not her anymore. Some other voice comes out of her mouth . . . she even walks differently."

"What does she say?"

"She hates it. She told me yesterday that this god has been after her for a long time, and she kept saying no because of the children. He won't wait any longer, she says. If she won't agree to be his *tang-ki*, something bad will happen to her or to one of her children." Wu Chieh spoke as if she needed to convince me, that if I "understood" then it would be okay. I was not willing to take on that responsibility, but I wanted to know what was happening. We had not been talking many minutes when a very skinny, very worried-looking little boy appeared in the door and said, "Wu Chieh. A-bu [Mother] wants you to come. She is acting funny again. Please come."

Wu Chieh turned pale and looked at me. Before I could venture an opinion, Lim A-pou, the senior woman in our household, appeared at the door and said, "Wu Chieh, Tan A-mei is calling for you. You had better go before she gets any worse. She wants you to take care of her kids. She says the god is after her again." A-pou turned to me and said, "She is drawing a big crowd down there. If you go to look, stay out of sight, or she will grab you and try to make you believe her."

"Ma-chi, please don't go."

"You just go take care of Mrs. Tan. I won't get into any trouble."

"Professor Wu would be very angry with me if anything happened . . ." A-cin began to pull on her skirt, and Wu Chieh reluctantly followed him out of the room and into the courtyard. I was both amused and irritated that this very young woman saw herself as "responsible" for me in the absence of my spouse.

I also realized that for the last half hour I had forgotten the weight of the hot, sodden air. It came back to me in full force as I went out the back door and made my way down the dusty path toward the Tan house. The sun reflected cruelly off the hard yellow earth path, and even when I turned into the shade of a large old tree that guarded the courtyard, there was relief only from the glare.

Lim A-pou was right. There must have been forty people in the usually empty yard. They were all focused on the spectacle in front of them and paid no attention at all to my presence. I leaned against a wall and opened my notebook to do the usual quick list of who was present. There were quite a few more women than men, and the men clumped together, trying to look casual. The women were in the groups that had now become familiar to me—divided by age and to some extent by the surnames of their husbands. The oldest women seemed to be gathered around the three most respected women of the village, two of whom were known for their piety, and the third for her diplomacy. The opinions of all three were frequently sought on everything from marriage negotiations to local politics.

Tan A-mei was kneeling in the center of the yard in full sun. She had a handful of burning incense sticks and was speaking in a deep singsong voice. The language was Hokkien, but I couldn't understand a word of it. I asked a young woman standing next to me what she was saying, and she replied, "Who can say? It is the god talking, and he isn't ready yet." Her mother-in-law turned to her and said, "Maybe. Maybe not. She can't even say who the god is, just that he has a face that is half black and half white." She turned to me. "She sent her mother to Banchiao to buy the god's image so that she could burn incense to him, but she wouldn't say his name. Only that the god said to go to a store on a particular street, and she would find the image." I asked her if this was the god that wanted to possess her, but apparently I got the language wrong, because the older woman suddenly gave me a sharp look and said, "Who knows." She moved off to join another bunch of women.

Her daughter-in-law, a woman in her early thirties who was already at war with her husband's mother, was happy to answer my questions, but before I got much more information, Mrs. Tan jumped to her feet and ran over to a group of women from one of the Lim households and began speaking loudly and boldly, standing with her feet apart and her elbows out, like a warrior in a country opera. "You have been having troubles in your family these last few weeks, but they are nearly over. Yesterday something good happened, and that is only the beginning. Your son's illness is about over. When you go home, you will find that his fever is nearly gone." The women at first looked embarrassed and then shocked.

The young woman next to me whispered that she had heard from the youngest daughter-in-law in the household that yesterday one of her husband's brothers had gotten a white-collar job in a new factory going up in Tamsui. "Nobody was supposed to know yet. How do you suppose she knows . . . unless . . ." She quickly turned to join the group her mother-in-law was in, whispering her exciting piece of gossip. From my position against the wall, I could watch this piece of information literally spread through the crowd.

Tan A-mei was not done with the Lims, however. After lapsing back into guttural nonsense syllables for a while, she turned to the woman with whom she had had a falling-out over the children's quarrels and said in a strong angry male voice, "You are the source of your family's ill fortune these last few months. I cannot help you. Offer a pig's head to Shang Ti Kung. He may be able to save your husband." The woman looked terrified and ran from the yard, pushing people out of her way.

At this point, Tan A-mei's mother returned, looking hot and flustered from her journey and dismayed at finding the large crowd surrounding her daughter. She searched out her son-in-law and berated him roundly for not taking better care of her. He looked sheepish and shrugged his shoulders. A-mei had fallen to her knees again, bowing and mumbling, still holding on to her sticks of incense. As her mother pulled her to her feet and tried to get her into the house, A-mei pushed free of her and turned to the crowd, shouting again in the god's voice, "You must all go home now and lock your doors. This evening I will visit some of you and prophesy." Then she slumped against her mother, who quickly led her into the house. I caught a glimpse of Wu Chieh in the house carrying the three-year-old on her back with the five-year-old clinging to her skirt.

When it seemed that the action was over, the men and some of the women began to straggle out of the yard. I hung around trying to pick up bits of conversation. Finally, as the crowd thinned out, I joined the group of older women, some of whom had settled comfortably on some large stones under the big tree. One of them was saying, "This morning when I was doing laundry, I heard her yelling, and I thought she was having a fight with Tien-lai—and who wouldn't have a fight with that worthless dog. But when I listened closely, I realized she was saying, "No, no, no. I won't accept you. Go away, leave me alone. I am just a poor mother." She went on and on like that until finally her mother calmed her down. That's when she promised to go get the black-and-white-faced god. Never heard of such a god. Maybe I'll go ask at the temple tomorrow . . ."

"A-thou, how do you know it's a god? This is the Seventh Month, after all. Have you thought of that? This wouldn't be the first time a ghost tried to possess someone, and women are weaker . . ."

"My old man says it is all nonsense. She's crazy, and they should keep her locked up until she gets better."

"Well, I was talking with Cui-tho, and he said he thought Tien-lai got the notion that if he could get people to believe she was a *tang-ki*, he could take her to Taipei and make big money at one of the temples."

"That man is too much! Would he do that to the mother of his sons?"

Before anyone could answer, loud sobs issued from the Tan house, and the women exchanged looks of concern and curiosity. At last, old So-cu hobbled over to the doorway on her gnarled bound feet and asked, "What's wrong here? Is there anything we can do?"

A-mei's mother stepped out the door, wringing her hands and looking genuinely miserable. "I had to tell her. Now she thinks she will surely die."

"What did you tell her, woman? Speak sense."

"I found the image just where she said it would be, but they wanted four hundred dollars for it. We don't have that kind of money. I don't even know how they paid for the hospital."

"How much have you got?"

"I have three hundred dollars and some change."

"Huh." So-cu reached in her pocket, pulled out several wrinkled dirty bills, and slowly smoothed them out with her arthritic fingers. "That's fifty dollars," she said and turned to look at the other women—not exactly expectantly but not quite blankly either. After some muttering and fumbling in pockets, the other fifty dollars was raised, and A-mei's mother turned and called to her daughter somewhere in the darkened house, "A-mei, A-mei, your friends and neighbors have given us money to buy the god figure. See how much they respect you?" There was only silence from within the house, and then Wu Chieh came out and said, "She has gone to sleep."

One of the old women noted for her religious activity gave So-cu a knowing look, and So-cu said gruffly, "Doesn't mean a thing. It's hot, and I want my nap too. There is no god calling me."

"So-cu, you are the limit. If you don't believe in her god, why did you give her mother the money?"

"I am not saying I believe or don't believe. I'm just not in any big hurry. Maybe tomorrow I'll go over and chat with Ong Hue-lieng . . ." It was clear that the assembled women took this as a significant development, so as So-cu departed, leaning on her cane, I asked one of my companions who Ong Hue-lieng might be.

"Ong Hue-lieng knows everything. If he has never heard of A-mei's god, the god doesn't exist. He knows all the ordeals they use to see if it is a ghost who is after her or a god . . . that kind of thing. So-cu wouldn't bother him unless she thought something serious was going on."

A-mei's mother came out of the house carrying her sunshade and announced that she was off to buy the god for her daughter. The rest of us followed her out of the yard and went our separate ways. Great black clouds had appeared over the mountains to the east, and I thought I saw an occasional flash of lightning, but this had happened too many times in recent weeks for me to look at them with any anticipatory shivers. The short walk back to the house was an endurance contest. I realized that I was panting. Although it was not much cooler, my office was a welcome sight. Liang Chieh padded in with a glass of lukewarm tea and said irritably, "You shouldn't go there when it is this hot. No wonder that woman is crazy with all of you staring at her." I did not argue. Liang Chieh grumped around the office for a bit, hoping I would give her some choice bits of gossip, and finally gave up when I began to shuffle papers.

By evening, A-mei's god had been installed on a makeshift altar outside the door of her house. When I arrived around eight, there was already a crowd and an atmosphere of intense excitement. There was no noticeable drop in temperature, and the crowd in the yard made me slightly claustrophobic. Gioq-ki, a middle-aged woman who lived at the other end of the village, told me that she had been in the house earlier and smelled puffs of fragrant air. I must have looked puzzled, for her daughter explained politely that this was a sure sign a god was present. I asked her if she thought it was true. She smiled and said, "That is what my mother told me."

I had just changed position to get a better view of the god when A-mei came staggering out of the house, chanting loudly, and flailing her arms about. A-pou, the senior woman from my house, pulled me back a little and said, "You had better keep out of sight or she will be after you for sure. She keeps going up to people telling them what is wrong with them and what they should do. She would have a lot of fun with you." I thanked her and asked what had been happening.

"Well, about an hour ago, she caught poor A-hok as he was coming home from Tainan and accused him of stealing money from her. He hadn't heard anything about what had been going on, and I thought he was going to have a fit himself. He told her she was crazy and then looked up and saw this crowd watching . . . We all laughed-to-death. He turned red and hurried on down the path. A-mei looked confused, like she might cry. Then she went back in the house. She just now came back out."

A-mei called out the name of the neighbor she had been having trouble with. I saw the woman slip out of the crowd and go into her house, closing the door quietly behind her. A-mei searched the faces surrounding her and picked out a man who was known to be a kindly soul, although a bit lazy by village standards. "Ah, Thiam-ting, Thiam-ting, you are a good man. You gave my A-mei a ride home on your bicycle one rainy night. I thank you. You will have good fortune and many sons" (a play on his name, literally "Add Sons," which had always amused me, since it was unlikely that his middle-aged wife would give him more than the four they already had). A-mei rubbed his chest enthusiastically, and Thiam-ting looked painfully embarrassed. As soon as her attention shifted, he fled.

"Wu Ma-chi, Wu Ma-chi. Where is the foreign female big nose? Does she not believe in me?" A-pou gave me a sharp yank back into a doorway and stepped in front of me. Several people looked around but did not see me in the shadows. "Wu Ma-chi, why do you ask so many questions? Come to me, and I will give you all the answers. I know all the answers to your questions." She was roaming through the crowd with a vague, almost bored look on her face, but the voice she used was strong and intent. To my relief, her attention was caught by So-cu, seated on a stool with her hands folded over her cane. "So-cu, you too are very wise. You know my name, but you won't say it. Right? Right?" So-cu looked at her intently and said, "You tell me your name." A-mei gave a deep throaty laugh that was so threatening it made me feel like giggling and cringing at the same time. "Even you do not give orders to a god." So-cu smiled comfortably and gave A-mei a barely perceptible nod. I was impressed.

Suddenly A-mei began angrily shouting the name of the

troublesome neighbor, picked up a hoe handle, rushed through the crowd like a figure in a Chinese opera, and started banging on the closed (unusual in a Taiwanese village) door of her house. "Lian-hua, Lian-hua, Lian-hua. Come out. I know you are in there. Come out and explain your bad character to the god. If you value your children's lives, come and pay respect to the god." Several people in the crowd began to look anxious. One of the men leaned over and said something to Tien-lai, and he just shrugged his shoulders, but A-mei's mother came running out of the house and pulled on her daughter's arm. "Please, daughter, come home. Come home now. Your children are calling for you." She pleaded with her a bit longer, and finally A-mei turned, and looking around confusedly at the crowd, quietly followed her mother across the yard and into the house. She walked like a normal, if very weary, village woman with no trace of the arrogant male posture she had assumed for the last half hour. One of the women next to me whispered, "See, just like a *tang-ki*. The god has left her now." I could not hear her companion's answer, but the tone was doubtful.

The kids resumed chasing each other about the yard as their parents split into different knots of conversation. I went up to inspect the god more closely. It was a crudely carved standard god figure. Its only distinctive characteristic was the unusual face painting—black on one half and white on the other. One of the men who worked in Taipei told me he rode home on the same train with A-mei's mother, and the paint had still been wet. "Made-to-order god. If Tien-lai is going to make any money off of her, he will have to do better than this. At least get a decent statue and a flowery name for it." I asked him what he meant. "Why do you think Tien-lai just sits there and brags about the mysterious things she has been saying? You watch, he will figure out a way to start charging pretty soon."

Another man said, "Well, you can't be sure about these things. She knew some things about my brother's wife's fam-

ily that it would have been hard for anyone to find out." The
first man grinned cynically and moved away.

"She really is saying some curious things. I hear Ong
Hue-lieng is coming around in the morning. That will settle
things."

"What will he do?"

"Oh, he just knows how to talk to gods and that sort of
thing. He will know whether it's a ghost or a god or what's
wrong."

"What do you think?"

"How do I know? I'm just a country person. But some of
the old women (he used a respect term) say they smelled the
fragrant air in the house. One can't put too much over on
them."

I wandered around a bit longer, picking up bits of conversation, trying to assess village opinion. There was a lot of
disagreement. With a number of important exceptions, more
women than men seemed to believe a supernatural of some
sort was after A-mei, but only a few were totally convinced.
Most of the believers or would-be believers were waiting for
Ong Hue-lieng's visit before they said any more. I saw So-cu
shake her head and walk slowly, painfully, out of the yard. I
wondered what the significance, if any, of that might be. As I
moved out of the yard toward home, I was amused to find
that two food sellers, having discovered a crowd, had set up
their carts. They located crowds, hence business, as inevitably
as mosquitoes.

Our rooms were still unbearably hot when I got home, so I
joined other members of the family out on the veranda. It
wasn't much cooler, but the air seemed less used up. Lim
Han-cu handed me a cigarette, and we sat and smoked in
silence for a while. I finally got up the nerve to ask him once
again what he thought about the events in the other end of
the village. He chuckled and said, "Ah, Ma-chi, there are
things none of us can understand. When I was a boy, I
laughed at the people who carried the gods in their chairs

across beds of hot coals, and then it came time for my family to do it. They were real coals, all right. I didn't get burned because I obeyed my father's instructions, but father's older brother's son carried scars to his grave because he slept with his wife the night before." He paused and laughed self-consciously. "When I was a young man, I laughed at people who talked about seeing ghosts. Then late one night I saw my neighbor's mother coming home for her feastday—she had been dead for ten years. So, now I don't laugh at anything anymore. I'm not saying I believe everything the priests or the *tang-ki* say, but I don't scorn it either."

"Some people tell me Tan Tien-lai thinks he can make money if his wife becomes a *tang-ki* . . ."

"That's true. He probably could. He probably could even if the god wasn't calling her as long as she was willing to act the part."

"Do you think she might be crazy?"

"She certainly acts crazy . . . *tang-ki* are supposed to act crazy, or nobody would believe the god was in them."

I laughed and said, "Lim Han-cu, you are not going to tell me what you think, are you?"

"I don't know what to tell you. Go talk to So-cu. When she makes up her mind, she will tell the other women, and they will tell their old men, and then we will all know what to think."

"Ong Hue-lieng is coming tomorrow, they say."

"Yes."

"Will So-cu make up his mind for him too?"

"Or he will give words to her thoughts."

I gave up. Lim Han-cu probably really didn't know what to make of Tan A-mei's behavior. I'd suspected more than once that when he couldn't answer one of our questions authoritatively, he spoke in riddles to keep us impressed. Most of the time I was impressed without the riddles—he was an intelligent man who was more analytic of his culture than any of his fellow villagers.

Later, as I slid under the mosquito net, hoping to fall asleep before the sheets were totally drenched with sweat, I realized that Lim Han-cu *was* telling me something. He wasn't speaking in riddles. Perhaps what he was telling me was how age can erase gender in the constantly shifting sands of power; perhaps he was also telling me something about the interaction between the supernatural world and the social world. So-cu was a specialist in one; Ong Hue-lieng was a specialist in the other. I would have given anything to be in on their conversation, but knew that it would not be the same conversation if I were. I drifted into a troubled sleep.

Liang Chieh and I were nearly through breakfast before Wu Chieh stumbled in. She looked at my coffee and asked if she could have a cup. "Of course," I said. Liang Chieh looked disapproving as she poured a mug full and dumped in several spoons of sugar. Although only nineteen, Wu Chieh had a good many strands of white hair, probably as the result of persistent malnutrition as a child. Liang Chieh insisted it was because she had eaten too much foreign food. Liang Chieh would not allow any foreign fare save coffee and an occasional loaf of bread in the house. She was particularly unhappy when Wu Chieh drank coffee.

"When did you finally get home?"

"She calmed down around midnight. They had some pills the doctor had given them, but Tan Tien-lai won't let her take them in the daytime."

"What was she doing?"

"Talking silly talk."

"Have you decided whether it's a god or a ghost that is after her?"

Wu Chieh threw me a quick look to see if I was making fun of her and apparently decided I was serious.

"How would I know? Maybe this morning when Ong Hue-lieng comes . . ."

"Have you talked with So-cu?"

"No, well, yes. She came around a couple of times yesterday and asked me some questions, but she didn't answer any."

"What kind of questions?"

"Just about stuff A-mei was doing when she was in the house."

"What did you tell her?"

"There wasn't much to tell her. She sleeps a lot, and then she talks nonsense, and then she talks in the god's voice."

"How about when she is with the children?"

"So-cu asked that too. Why?"

"Just curious."

"Well, she really likes her children, and she wouldn't do anything to hurt them. She is just like usual with them."

"You mean if they come up to her when she is talking in the god's voice, she stops?"

"She always is whispering to them, even when she is okay. She just whispers a little more now. The kids aren't scared . . . only when she is outside running around."

"What about A-mei's mother? What does she think?"

"She is really worried—much more than Dumb Tien-lai. She wants to get a better doctor. She wants her to take the pills the doctor gave her. And she is always trying to get her to eat more. She wants to take her home, but Tien-lai won't let her."

"Does she think a god is trying to make her his *tang-ki?*"

"Mainly she is worried about her health. She says, 'Whatever it is, she needs to rest and not have all this commotion.' "

"Wu Chieh, does she think this god she bought wants to use her daughter as a medium?"

"She is very devout."

"Uh-huh . . ." I waited, trying to hold her to the question with my attention.

"I heard her tell So-cu that as a little girl she often went to the temples in Keelung to talk with the gods there."

"Really? Do many little kids do that?"

"I never did."

"When will Ong Hue-lieng come?"

"Who knows? Some time today . . ."

Wu Chieh settled down to the steaming bowl of congee

Liang Chieh had served her and answered the rest of my questions with stubborn monosyllables. Liang Chieh finally told me to lay off. She tried to distract me with the latest weather report. They were predicting that the typhoon moving fast across the South Pacific *might* bring rain and some cooler weather within the next few days. We rolled our eyes at each other, having heard this same promise several times in the last miserable weeks. I wandered off to the office to see if there was anything I might have missed in the month-old *Time* magazine.

An hour later, just as I was beginning to wonder if Wu Chieh was going to report to work at all today, I heard her *zori* slip-slopping across the courtyard.

Without any greeting or explanation, she blurted out, "When they were doing laundry this morning at the riverbed, So-cu told A-mei's mother that she should take her to a better doctor." Wu Chieh was agitated and upset.

"So?"

"Well, it is like she has made up her mind. Ong Hue-lieng hasn't even come yet . . ."

"Did she come right out and *say* she thought A-mei was mentally ill?"

"No, but she wouldn't. I don't see why everyone listens to her. What makes her so special?"

"What did A-mei's mother say?"

"I don't know. I wasn't there."

"I mean what did she say to you?"

"She was asking me about So-cu, mainly. Most of the time she seems anxious and worried, but this morning she just seemed really sad."

"Did you see A-mei?"

"No, but I heard her in the bedroom, chanting stuff. Her mother said she did that most of the night. They are all really tired."

"Where is Tan Tien-lai?"

"I saw him down at the store talking to some of the men.

He was telling them to come around when Ong Hue-lieng comes. You know Mrs. Kho, the storekeeper's wife?"

"Uh-huh."

"She told me that Tien-lai was asking people for contributions so that he could make better offerings for A-mei's god. He was telling people that he was afraid the god was getting insulted because this village hadn't held a feast for him yet. She said she didn't know how much he got elsewhere, but she had seen him pick up close to two hundred dollars yesterday from people sitting around the store."

"Did he make better offerings?"

"Not really. You know, he even talked Mrs. Kho into giving him incense sticks for her. She thinks he uses the money to gamble." Wu Chieh seemed to calm down as she "reported" to me, but after a pause, she blurted out, her voice full of misery, "Ma-chi, I *know* A-mei doesn't know anything about the money. I *know* she isn't acting this way for money. She hates it. She wants to be like everybody else. She hates to have everybody staring at her. She wants her neighbors to treat her with respect and to be able to take care of her kids . . ." She seemed to run out of steam and finally said, almost whining, "Ma-chi, I don't want to go back. Do I have to go down there again?"

"I thought you wanted to. No, you don't need to go."

"But you want to know what's happening."

"That's true, but we can find out from other people. How come you don't want to go back?"

"I just don't."

"Did she frighten you?"

"No. Of course, not. It's just . . ."

I couldn't tell whether she was struggling for the right words or a way to avoid answering my question so I just sat, concentrating on the rivulet of sweat trailing down my backbone. We both fell into our own thoughts, and I was so far gone that I jumped slightly when Wu Chieh finally broke the silence.

"Well, I guess I want to be there when Ong Hue-lieng comes; and if she starts dancing again, the children get upset, so I should be there."

"Really, Wu Chieh, it is up to you."

"Yes. I am going to go."

"Well, I'll be wandering around talking to people, so if you decide to come back here and forget about it, it is okay with me." I made a mental note to tell her about some of my religious disappointments . . . some other time.

"You shouldn't try to come into the Tan house, you know. You would upset her."

"Okay, I'll stay out of sight."

Wu Chieh trailed on out again, stuffing her tiny pad of paper into her skirt pocket. I shook my head in wonder at the realization that somehow in the past year we had turned this naive nineteen-year-old with a minimal middle-school education into a budding social scientist. Or had we simply found an unusually bright young woman with a well-organized mind who had as much curiosity about the world around her as we did? Whichever, right now she was in conflict, and there was little I could do to help. She had made it clear that it was not my decision.

I settled at my desk to write some letters before the dense heat drained me of the ability to write the cheerful newsy pages necessary each month to keep my anxious family at peace. Before I got the first page written, a small head poked around my door and said shyly, "Sister Wu sent me to tell you that . . . that . . . that old man had arrived." He delivered his message, whoever he was, and dashed out of the courtyard. Whether he was afraid of me or of my landlord's children (who were considered fierce), or was simply in a big hurry to get back to the action, I would never know, for he was out of sight before I could get out of my chair. I put the cardboard box over the typewriter, found my sunglasses, and went out the door, exchanging the dim dense heat of indoors for the dull glare of intense sun filtered through a blanket of sodden air. I couldn't believe that I could feel any hotter, but I was wrong.

I was surprised to find a much smaller crowd of people in the yard than had been around the last few days—certainly smaller than last night. A couple of women I didn't recognize were burning incense and praying in front of the altar. In the daylight, the god looked even shabbier than it had before. The paint job was amateurish, or maybe just uncertain. They had not gotten their money's worth, if indeed the entire four hundred dollars had been spent on the god. Two or three of the younger women were peering in the front door of the house, where, I was told by one of my neighbors, Ong Hue-lieng was talking to A-mei and her family in front of the ancestral tablets. I was surprised to see So-cu and another of the older women on the far side of the yard washing vegetables at the village well as if nothing was happening. I asked my neighbor, who drove a pedicab in Tapu when he was not needed for farm work, what he thought was going on.

"Not much. Old Ong just came over to put an end to it. She's crazy, and that god is just a doll somebody sold them."

"How do you know? Yesterday everyone seemed to think she might be a *tang-ki*."

"Not everyone. Lots of people are like ducks. If they see one duck jump in the river, then they jump in too. Some people look before they jump."

"Did anything happen yesterday to change people's minds?"

"Got me. I worked late last night—weekends are good for business. By the time I got up this morning, nobody seemed particularly interested anymore. I guess they're interested in what will happen next but not excited. What do you think?"

I shrugged my shoulders diplomatically and was saved from an answer by a commotion at the door to the Tan house. The women moved back, and Ong Hue-lieng came out with an irritated look on his face. He turned to the women but took in everyone else within hearing and said, "Why don't you go about your business and leave this poor woman in peace. She is sick and she needs some rest." With that he hurried out of the yard without looking right or left. A-mei's mother, who attempted to "see him off" as Taiwanese courtesy requires, hadn't gotten halfway across the courtyard before he was out of sight. Her social discomfort was obvious, but she also looked relieved—at the departure of Ong Hue-lieng or at the results of his meeting with them? Tien-lai, who by rights should have ushered out the guest, was nowhere in sight.

The men in the yard began to drift off, but the women closed around A-mei's mother like birds on an unattended bowl of rice. I hesitated, mindful of my promise to Wu Chieh, but before I could decide, Tan Tien-lai called to his mother-in-law from inside the house in less than respectful tones. She looked angry and said to the women, "I'd better talk to him for my daughter's sake." She went in, and as some of the women moved toward the entrance of the house, a red-faced and angry Tien-lai slammed and barred the double doors. One of the women smiled and said, "I bet it gets hot in there." The other women laughed and began to gather up their laundry, the vegetables to be washed for the noon meal, or whatever they had in their hands when the word had gotten out of Ong Hue-lieng's arrival.

I considered going over to talk with So-cu, but found she was no longer at the well. I wandered on home, stopping along the way to watch some children playing Chinese hopscotch and to buy matches at the store. The sun was on the loungers' bench in front of the store so there was no one around. Mrs. Kho's youngest daughter, a thirteen-year-old who could add up the prices for a half dozen items and make change like the fastest cash register, was incapable of answering the simplest question without dissolving into embarrassed giggles (we called it the early-teenager syndrome). She was the only person in the store, so I took my matches and left.

Wu Chieh didn't come home for lunch. She sent a child to tell Liang Chieh not to wait for her. We ate gloomily. Liang

Chieh had heard that the storm was moving up the straits from Hong Kong, but neither of us believed the weather forecasts, local or U.S. military, any longer. After lunch, I wandered back to the office, looking with distaste at my unfinished letter, and searched around for a novel that hadn't been read too recently. About three o'clock, I heard first one and then a second pedicab on the path leading out of the village. They weren't rattling, and they were moving slowly, evidence that they were occupied. About an hour later, one came back rattling emptily and then departed again, heavily laden. My neighbor was doing a good business today, but I didn't envy him peddling a loaded pedicab on that long bumpy path during the hottest part of the afternoon.

Not long after, the slip-slop of Wu Chieh's *zori* announced her return home. I heard Liang Chieh imperiously ordering her to eat some lunch, but within minutes she arrived at my door with an orange in her hand. She looked terrible.

"They've gone."

"Who is gone?"

"Tan A-mei, her mother, and the children."

"Where to?"

"Home."

"For a rest?"

"Tien-lai says he will go Monday morning either to get divorce papers or papers to commit her to a hospital where they lock up crazy people."

"Oh dear."

"He won't. He is too lazy. Besides, as long as they are at his mother-in-law's, he doesn't have to worry about feeding them."

"How was she?"

"Her mother gave her a bunch of pills, so she was hardly awake. I'm going to go take a nap. Okay?"

"Best thing you could do. Don't you want something to eat first?"

She shook her head and left.

Wu Chieh slept until dinnertime, announced that she was going into Tapu to see a movie with a couple of the other unmarried women in the village, and hurried out. I was vaguely aware of her return in the late evening, but decided not to talk with her until the next day.

About midnight, the wind began, and by two o'clock rain so heavy I thought it would surely crush the roof began to pour from the sky. The wind ripped and tore around the house, and I could hear loose objects clattering across the village with an occasional crash as one of them connected with a more substantial object. By four, the roar of the river could be heard over the pounding of the rain as the runoff from Taiwan's steep mountains raced back to the sea. For the first time in a month, I looked for a sheet to pull over me.

Armed Forces News Bulletin

Taipei, Taiwan, July 15, 1960

A flash flood resulting from Typhoon Lily totally washed away the small village of Peihotien with great loss of life. Survivors claim that a local god called down the flood as punishment for nonbelievers. An American woman living in the village is among the missing. Rescue workers are on the scene.

Commentary

There was a time—and not so long ago—that publishing "The Hot Spell" would have cast a shadow of doubt, a questioning of legitimacy, over my mainstream anthropological publications. In part, this was because of my unorthodox career; in part because of my gender. "The Hot Spell" is clearly labeled fiction; my first ethnography, *The House of Lim* (1968), was clearly labeled "a study." Nonetheless, several times during the year or two following the publication of that work (while I was still an anthropologist's wife), I was complimented on my recently published "novel." Clifford is quite right when he suggests that "groups long excluded from positions of institutional power" (1986: 21, n. 11) less commonly publish "experimental texts" because they are more likely than white men to be untenured. But the relationship between gender and experimentation is more complex than a mere concern about academic security. As Caplan points out, "When women were using the experiential approach to ethnographic writing, much of it was dismissed as 'self-indulgence' . . . ; now that it is being done by men, it is called 'experimental,' perhaps an example of what Judith Okely . . . has termed the 'curious shift of meaning' which tends to attach to correlations when gender is added" (1988: 16). In other words, men explore new paradigms; women mess around on the fringes of knowledge/art/literature/whatever.

With all the interest that the work of Clifford et al. and their critics has created, it is interesting that almost without exception, the anthropologist who makes an experimental contribution does so after first publishing his or her standard monograph. (See Marcus 1986: 265–66 for a slightly different observation on this ordering.) This may be a time of transition, which is to say, in the future more experimental texts may be firstborns, but I doubt whether many anthropologists will be willing to give up the realist text totally. The reasons are several: a lack of clarity on just who the audience for experimental ethnography might be, a recognition that a realist text—whatever its problems—will be more valued by and valuable to the discipline, and perhaps an uncomfortable feeling that this excessive authorial presence just *might* make the text seem a bit self-indulgent. How accurate my suspicions are about extant experimenters and the ordering of their texts is another paper (and another author), but experimental texts thus far (e.g., Crapanzano 1980; Dwyer 1982; Obeyesekere 1981; Rabinow 1977; Schieffelin 1976) have been praised more for being experimental than for the new insights they provided into the culture. Indeed, the less generous critics suggest that readers find out more about the self than the other (e.g., Roth 1989: 557).

So why is there so much interest, then, in experimenting with ethnographic form, at least theoretically? (The actual number of innovative texts published by anthropologists in the last decade is limited—perhaps ten to fifteen, depending on who is defining "innovative.") Obviously, this is a question that can be answered in several contexts—politically, academically, and intellectually. Within philosophy, literary criticism, and the humanities in general, there has been a major (or some would insist minor) questioning of the epistemological foundations of nearly everything in recent years. Anthropology is a discipline with very permeable borders, picking up methodologies, theories, and data from any source whatever that can provide the answers to our questions, so it is not surprising that what has come to be labeled postmodernism should be welcomed, at least by a vocal few (Caplan 1988: 9), and translated into a critique of traditional as well as interpretive ethnography. What is "surprising" to feminist anthropologists is how many of the postmodern criticisms that are now of such interest to the discipline were ignored or treated with amused tolerance when we originally voiced them (Caplan 1988: 10; Gordon 1988: 7–24; Mascia-Lees et al. 1989: 11). I am thinking in particular of the recognition of the effect of personal/political/ethnic biases on our research, of the need to rethink our ways of presenting the experience of the "other," and of the extent to which such a representation is even possible.

Feminists from all disciplines have been examining their own work and that of their male colleagues for nearly three decades in order to identify the biases we bring not only to our methods but to the very research questions we ask. As third-world feminists have found their own voices, feminist anthropologists internationally have become painfully aware of the remnants of a colonial mind-set in their research. We have begun to search for a way to do ethnographic research that not only will not exploit other women but will have positive effects on their lives. Feminist anthropologists are struggling with ways of transforming the objects of research into *subjects*, who themselves identify and design the research projects *they* think are needed, who retain control over the written outcome of the research, and who jointly publish with the anthropologists (Caplan 1988: 9; Mascia-Lees et al. 1989: 33). Feminist anthropologists are aware of the difficulties involved in such collaborative endeavors, perhaps more so than the postmodernists who so cheerfully encourage the idea. As Frances Mascia-Lees and her colleagues put it, "Our suspicion of the new ethnographer's desire for collaboration with the 'other' stems not from any such refusal to enter into dialogue with that 'other,' but from our history and understanding of being appropriated and literally spoken for by the dominant, and from our consequent sympathetic identification with the subjects of anthropological study in this regard" (1989: 21).

Probably the aspect of the postmodernist critique of ethnography that has most raised the ire of anthropologists is what Clifford himself called "our fetishizing of form" (1986:

21), the "our" being the seminar held at the School of American Research Seminar that resulted in *Writing Culture*. (The "form fetish" was one of the reasons the feminist critique was not considered relevant to their seminar, since our fetish is more content than form, according to Clifford. The point is arguable.) Even anthropologists who are prepared at least to question the degree to which the term science in social science is bad usage are uncomfortable about having the methods of textual criticism used to evaluate their work. As Michael Carrithers so nicely states it, "We cannot very fruitfully apply criteria useful in thinking about fiction to a different genre altogether. To do so is like trying to reach a judgment on significance of rhyme for Henry James: not an absolutely pointless exercise but at best a tangential one" (1990: 54).

Postmodernists are very concerned about anthropologists' control over their texts—the means by which they establish their legitimacy as authorities who are describing exotic but nonetheless existing realities. The postmodernist goal is, I take it, to encourage the author to present a less tidy picture with more contradictory voices and to encourage the reader to take more responsibility for puzzling out what is really going on in Wiliwililand. This last is a particularly sticky point. According to Clifford, "Recent literary theory suggests that the ability of a text to make sense in a coherent way depends less on the willed intentions of an originating author than on the creative activity of a reader" (1988b: 52). He goes on to point out the alternative readings to which an ethnographic text might be subjected, causing one to wonder if the authority of the author is really such a problem after all, except of course for the very people who would find the complexly written experimental ethnographies daunting anyway.

If anthropologists are appalled by the idea of using the methods of literary criticism to evaluate their work, they are even more nervous (with good reason) about calling fiction ethnography or even using the literary forms of fiction in ethnographic writing. To quote Carrithers once again, "Writers write fiction, and on our usual understanding fiction is not real, so to regard anthropologists as writers is to grant them intrinsic worth but to withdraw credence" (1990: 54). The threat to the believability of the work of a particular anthropologist who chooses to take the risk is one thing, but the threat to the discipline as a whole is quite another, a topic I will return to below.

As a number of doubters have suggested, fiction or even the use of the literary devices of fiction may serve to exacerbate rather than solve the problems for which they are recommended. Mascia-Lees and her colleagues have suggested that "authors who experiment with point of view, presenting a seeming jumble of perspectives and subjectivities in a variety of voices, may well be writing no more open texts than classic works in which all action is mediated by a unitary narrative voice" (1989: 30). Indeed, the anthropologist can more easily hide behind the voices of the "others" she has selected to speak or, if the work is fiction, created to speak for her. To my thinking, this puts us in more danger of appropriating the experience of the other than does the old-fashioned "me looking at them and telling you about it" mode.

"The Hot Spell" is certainly not an example of postmodernist fiction, for it makes no attempt at different points of view or perspectives—everything that happens is presented through the narrator's voice. It was written as fiction, not ethnography. It could be read as a "confessional tale" (à la Van Maanan 1988): the not-yet anthropologist talks about her boredom, her discomfort, her irritation with the local staff, her insecurity. For the same reasons, it could be read as a reflexive text: the narrator reveals her biases, her state of mind at the time of a dramatic set of events, and so forth. And it could be called dialogic: the author "allows" the competing voices to have their say. But it *was* written as fiction. The narrator's "confession" is artifice, with an eye to winning the reader's empathy if not sympathy. When one checks the dates against the fieldnotes in the next chapter, it becomes clear that the precipitating activities actually took place before the typhoon season, when the weather was likely to still be cool and damp—the author introduced an oppressive humid heat wave as a potential explanatory agent, another character in the play.

And in the final paragraph, she allows a totally undeveloped character, this mysterious black-and-white-faced god, to undermine the "realist" text. Was she confessing to "going native" along with all her other failings? Or is this veiled reflexivity? By suggesting that the "survivors" of the village catastrophe believed the god was punishing them, was the author simply using a literary device to unsettle a comfortable sense of closure—or was she attempting to show "the world observed as open-ended, ambiguous, and in flux" (Marcus & Cushman 1982: 45), a goal of experimental ethnography?

Since I am the author, I can answer that question with authority—I didn't want a tidy first-world ending. However, as Clifford notes, literary analysts don't take authorial intent very seriously these days. So perhaps this is unintentional reflexivity? Perhaps I/author was attempting to lead the reader to the conclusion that authorial authority is dangerous, that accepted truths about the nature of reality are flawed, and that closure is misleading. The point is that the sophisticated, or merely sensitive, reader may decide for herself whose authority she accepts—among those presented for her consideration. Graham Watson would object to the notion of unintentional reflexivity ("displays of reflexivity are not self-evidently such"; 1987: 36), but he, too, would be comfortable assigning more responsibility for interpretation to the reader: "It is not enough that writers stop hankering after authority; it is necessary also that readers stop requiring authoritative accounts from writers" (ibid.).

Watson qualifies this somewhat cranky statement when he

goes on to criticize an experimental piece of ethnography with the observation:

It bears reiterating that the reader consults an ethnographic text for news of the world conveyed to him by an accredited reporter.* If he suspects that news brought to him is conveyed, not by a qualified professional social scientist, but by a layman, then he will not warrant it as anthropology; he will deem it unsifted raw material of undetermined validity and significance. (1987: 36)

As Watson sees it, a reflexive ethnography that by definition causes the reader to question the anthropologist's authority is in fact a contradiction in terms but one we will simply have to live with. He is, alas, no more helpful in answering his own question of how one is to differentiate ethnograpy from fiction, other than in the preface, footnotes, and other authorial devices.

This is begging the question. An ethnographer is guided by certain rules of evidence—call them scientific if one must— that are assumed by her readers. Her competence in meeting these standards is another issue. A writer of fiction, however, has another set of rules—all she need do is tell a convincing story. The novelist or short story writer is in total control of the information presented, the attitudes and motives of her characters, and the sequence of events. She can even call down typhoons or the wrath of the gods. More important, she can, and in the case I have presented here does, cut off many alternative explanations for the events that she purports to describe. For example, the "I" and Wu Chieh in this story see a clique of senior women in Peihotien as controlling the decision about the cause of Mrs. Tan's behavior. The author

---

*Rather than littering the text with "sic" after each male pronoun implying that all anthropologists, authors, readers, and other humans are male, I let these pass without further comment. I find it ironic that scholars concerned about reflexivity are so oblivious to this obvious exclusionary device. I use "she" or "her" in place of the conventional "he/him" not to privilege the female voice but to call attention to the way in which the supposedly generic "he" does in fact privilege the male voice.

is under no obligation—indeed, it would interfere with the flow of the story—to explore all the other contradictory pressures that produced her aberrant behavior. The author of an ethnographic piece has another set of obligations. Carrithers, in his review of Clifford Geertz's *Works and Lives* (1988), makes this same point when he says:

Whereas the canon of a fictional realist might be to achieve verisimilitude, ethnographers adhere to quite a different standard. In their writing the touchstone must be fidelity to what they experienced and learned about others, and much of what they write has to be verifiably true ... a very different matter than the plausibility of inner harmony we ask of realist fiction. (1988: 22)

I chose to tell this story in the voice of a quasi-anthropologist. I could have used Wu Chieh as the "I," or So-cu, or even Mrs. Tan herself. For an anthropologist, this might have been an interesting and, no doubt, humbling exercise. Had I used Wu Chieh, the tale could have been more "confessional." I would surely have explored her attitudes toward the powerful foreigners (a penniless graduate student and his wife) and whatever ethical uneasiness she may have felt about passing on her observations on the personal life of her fellow Taiwanese. The story would probably have been focused more on her own struggle to come to terms with a supernatural experience. Had I taken Mrs. Tan as the narrator or focal character, the text could not have been typical realist fiction because she was under extraordinary stress and in contact with various "realities." I cannot remember now whether I even considered using these other voices, but I doubt it. I knew that I did not and could not think like a Taiwanese.

I can give my interpretation of what I see, hear, smell, and feel, filtered through a mind that was constructed in the United States. Even after many years of living in and doing research on Chinese society, I do not have the thought processes of one who was raised, socially constructed if you will, in China. I am not suggesting that only someone raised as a

Chinese can "really understand" Chinese culture, merely that some of the details that a Chinese telling this story would find important—convincing—I would probably miss.

Clifford points out:

> We need not ask how Flaubert knows what Emma Bovary is thinking, but the ability of the fieldworker to inhabit indigenous minds is always in doubt. Indeed this is a permanent, unresolved problem of ethnographic method. Ethnographers have generally refrained from ascribing beliefs, feelings, and thoughts to individuals. They have not, however, hesitated to ascribe subjective states to cultures. (1988b: 47)

Later in this paragraph, it becomes clear that the "subjective states" of which he writes are not really ascribed to "cultures" but ascribed to the Nuer as a people. In other words, the anthropologist makes generalizations about, say, the Nuer sense of time—a somewhat different matter, I would think, and in fact part of our analytic responsibility.

One of the things that troubles me most about the postmodernist stance is the retreat it promotes from the admittedly messy stuff of experience. If our ethnographies become polyvocal, somehow managing to portray all the uncertainties, inanities, complexities, and contradictions we encounter in our field research, we may indeed avoid appropriating the experience of our informants, but have we fulfilled the responsibility to our audience? Perhaps as Watson suggests, readers should stop demanding a holistic picture from us. But then why do we bother going "there" in the first place, if not to come back with "the news?"

When I was a girl growing up in a working-class family, I read everything I could get my hands on, but I was particularly interested in novels about women. I read to find out about a life that I saw from a distance but to which I had no access. I knew the stories were often "phony," but I didn't care. I wanted to know how women in cities boarded streetcars, bought food, chose their friends, what they talked about, and so on. And I wanted to know from someone who was there, had experienced it. I sometimes laughed at the plots (and sometimes I didn't understand them), but I hungered for the details they provided me on a life that seemed exotic and exciting. In time, though, I gave up on novels—there was no longer enough new information to make up for all the boring stories. That, I fear, may be the ultimate fate of experimental ethnography. Whether or not fictional accounts have more staying power will probably depend upon the skills of the authors, but the story line in novels will probably draw more readers. The story in this chapter does not do a quarter of the work that the essay in Chapter Four does in conveying information, analysis, and understanding about gender, shamanism, and power relations in a Chinese community, but it is, to use a sadly worn word, evocative. Fiction can evoke a setting, a social context, an involvement of all the senses in ways that enhance understanding. But it is no substitute for a well-written ethnographic account, and I don't see how it saves us from our colonial inclinations.

Anthropologists do fieldwork by themselves, by and large, or with a spouse, but very rarely in conjunction with other anthropologists. There may be restudies, and there may be studies in nearby villages, but in the main the individual anthropologist takes responsibility for and essentially promises her public that she will not only tell the truth as she knows it, but will check and recheck what villagers tell her about the way things are in that village. Amazing though it may seem, we simply assume that we all do this because it is part of the ethics of our profession: a slender thread of trust sustaining a heavy burden of credibility.

It seems to me that if the firm boundaries between fiction and ethnography are allowed to blur, we weaken the value of ethnographic research and gain little in exchange. We will have blurred the ethical assumptions of our craft, and our audience may come to wonder whether we have in any particular instance sacrificed a set of observations in order to preserve a mood or advance the plot—in other words, given precedence to form over content. In the end, our readers will have no basis to judge whether they are reading about a culture very different from their own or whether they are reading the product of a mind very different from their own, or both.

CHAPTER THREE

Fieldnotes

WHAT FOLLOWS are fieldnotes in almost the same form that they were recorded in 1960. The dates refer to the day they were typed. This was usually the same day the observation was made or the interview was given, but not always. This particular set of notes has a few confusions in dates that result from the way they were gathered. As I explained in Chapter One, Wu Chieh, our field assistant, did the majority of the fieldwork on this event, and she reported her "findings" to us while she was under personal pressure. I have not rearranged the notes to provide a perfect chronology because the point of including the "raw" data is to allow readers to surmise for themselves what in fact happened. In the Commentary that follows, I will explore some of the difficulties of recovering "reality" from such materials.

Since we were living with a large farm family whose members wandered in and out of our rooms, as we did theirs, and since we, as foreigners, were a source of considerable interest to the local police, we decided to assign numbers to all our informants and to use those numbers exclusively in our fieldnotes. This would, we hoped, provide some protection to our informants should our notes be confiscated, a very real possibility in that period of Taiwan's history. In order to give the reader some basic information about who is speaking or being spoken about, I have added the person's sex (F/M) and age in parentheses when they are first introduced in the text and elsewhere where necessary for clarity. Punctuation has also been added here and there, but beyond that I have retained errors and inconsistencies that were introduced at the time the notes were originally recorded.

March 5, 1960
Present: 153 (F 54), 154 (F 31), 254 (F 53), 189 (F 50), 230 (F 17)

Yesterday 48 (F 30) was taken by her husband to a mental hospital in Tapu. 481 (F 12) told Wu Chieh that the woman ran out into the field, and her husband had to come to pick her up and take her to the hospital. The women were talking about this today and said that she was sent to a big mental hospital, and that her husband went there to see her but was not allowed to see her because she was tied up. The doctor said there was nothing else he could do with her. Someone told Wu Chieh that something like this had happened to 48 once before, but she was not hospitalized then. The women say that her illness this time came about as the result of her worrying about losing NT$90. She couldn't find the money and asked 49 (her seven-year-old son) about it, and he told her that his father took it to gamble. Her husband said that this was not true. They said that she may have known that she was going to get sick, because the day before she took her baby (3 months) over to her sister's house and asked her to take care of the baby. They said that 47 (her 32-year-old husband) was very dumb. If he knows that his wife has this kind of illness, he should not let her worry. He should have said that he had taken the money even if he didn't. Instead, when she started to get sick, he stood there and told everyone, "She is going to go crazy, she is going to go crazy." The women said that this is the reason 47 is called "Dumb Tien-lai." 154: "When 492's (F 28) children and 48's children got into a fight and 48 went to talk with 492 about it, 492 scolded 48. She said: 'If children fight and kill each other it serves them right. If your children get killed, then you come and take your children home and bury them. You don't need to come and talk to me about it.' But once when 48's child hit 492's child, 492 went out and said something to 48, and she just said this back to her and then she had nothing to say." (All of the women agreed that 492 had said this to 48.)

Wu Chieh heard that 47 is going to go ask T'ai Tzu Yeh [a god] to help his wife get well. The women also said that when 48 fell into the field, she lay there saying: "Just because of children's things other people bully me, other people bully me just because of children's things. I won't forget this. I won't forget this." The women said that when a person is like this, you shouldn't let them worry and should encourage them to sleep a lot.

March 11, 1960

Wu Chieh talked with 48's mother who lives in Keelung.

Mother: "Before she was married, this happened to her once. I gave her to another family to be an adopted daughter, but they didn't treat her very well and sent her out to be a cook or servant for another family. She didn't like this and something else happened [the family she worked for scolded her or there was something of a sexual nature involved], and so she came running back to me. But I had to send her back to her adopted family, and it was then that this happened. She was thinking about all of this too much. After she got well, her adoptive mother sent her back and didn't want her anymore. Later she married 47, and this never happened again until now. That was over ten years ago, and it should not have happened again. It must be because someone did something to hurt her."

Wu Chieh: "Why do you think this happened this time?"

Mother: "They say that it is because she lost $90 that she had

saved for a *hwei* [private loan association meeting]. She had
$100 and spent $10 of it and then sat down by the river to
wash clothes. Either she lost the remaining money there or
someone stole it. She is the kind of person who cannot get
little things out of her mind, so when this happened she worried and worried about it. The one who hurt her (the one who
stole the money) ought to get an illness that is even worse
than hers. Once because the children got into a fight, 154
(F 31) scolded her and said: 'You are going to go crazy and
take off your clothes,' and lots of things like that. People
shouldn't scold one another like this just because children get
into a fight, because they get over it right away. The one who
gets scolded like this will keep thinking and thinking about it
and get very angry. Now she (48) is talking about one of the
children who died when she was nine months old. She kept
saying: 'It's because of her. It's because of her.' [This is a suggestion that the child's ghost is returning to "ask for something" from the living.] "So I told her that I would go and
bai-bai to the child,* and she said, 'No, no.' She told me that
we must buy an image and *bai-bai* to her. All I could do was
say all right, all right."

She asked Wu Chieh, "Could this really happen? The child
was only nine months old." She thought about it for a minute
and then answered herself, "It might if you have really bad
luck, and my daughter has really bad luck."

At this point 47 came in and told Wu Chieh that when they
took 48 to the hospital in Tapu, all they had done at the hospital was tie her up and give her some pills to make her go to
sleep. She apparently struggled a lot, as he also said that she
tore the skin off her wrists and broke a bed in the hospital.
48's mother asked 47 what 48 was like the first day. 47: "She

---

* *Bai-bai* can be used as a noun to describe the entire ritual associated with
offerings of food, incense, and paper money to various gods, as well as the feast-
ing that follows major festivals. The term is also used as a verb describing the
slight bowing over hands that are palm on palm, much like the Western Protes-
tant prayer position

just kept trying to run away, saying that she wanted to go and see you. That's all."

Wu Chieh says that the family went to ask [the god] Wu Nien Ch'ing Swei for some herbs. The family thinks that it is because 48 has a "fever in her heart" that she keeps beating herself on the chest and breaking the bed. 174 (F 66) also gave the family an herb which is supposed to reduce the heart fever. Wu Chieh says she watched 48 beating herself violently over her heart. 48 said that she had to *bai-bai* to "the god who crossed the ocean." Her mother didn't know who the god was until someone told her the story of Shang Ti Kung's returning for his birthday, and she said that it must be Shang Ti Kung that she means. 48's mother then told 47 to go and invite the god to the house and 174 said that it only costs one dollar a day.

Later that afternoon the family called in a Shang Ti Kung *tang-ki* (someone we have not seen around here before).

Wu Chieh asked 48's mother what the god had told them. 48's mother said: "He just said that she had met a ghost." She went on to say to Wu Chieh: "She is a very nice girl, my daughter. How can this kind of terrible thing happen to her? She is not a bad girl."

Wu Chieh said that today the family had both Wang Yeh and Shang Ti Kung in the house. She also noticed that 492 (F 28) did not go to see 48 the way most of the other village women did.

March 12, 1960

This afternoon 47 was telling a group of men that this noon his wife 48 had jumped out of bed and run around the house jumping up and down saying that the god was in her body, and that she had to buy the god's image to *bai-bai* to. At first the family just kept saying, "All right, all right," but when 48 didn't calm down and kept insisting that they buy a god, the family gave in and went to buy a god. As soon as she saw them go out to buy the god, 48 calmed down. 153 (F 54) and 48's mother then went to Taipei to buy a Shang Ti Kung for which they paid $350. Wu Chieh said that it was a clay figure of the god that doesn't cost as much as ones made of wood.

Later Wu Chieh overheard 47 telling all of the women that he knew that it wasn't true that the god was in her body. Wu Chieh commented that only 48's mother seemed to be really worried, while 47 seemed to greatly enjoy telling about the whole thing. 47 said to the women who had gathered in the yard in front of his house: "When I do something, I do it straight [never change my mind]. I am going to keep her here for one week and do everything I can to make her well, but if she isn't well in a week, then I am going to send her off to the hospital at Chang Su." One woman commented to another that 48 was getting better, and 47 interrupted: "No, it is very bad now. It is very bad now. At first she was yelling and hitting because the fever was in her heart, but now it has come up to her head [meaning now she is really crazy]." Wu Chieh asked 47 how he knew this, and he announced: "I'm a doctor. I'm a doctor." When she looked embarrassed, he went on, "Really. I am not joking. I can see it very clearly."

At this point 48's mother and 153 arrived from Taipei with the god they bought. They looked exhausted and hot. 47 went up to 48's mother and said: "See what I told you. Now she doesn't want it. She doesn't even want it."

Later, Wu Chieh asked 369 (F 24) about the god, and 369 said that 48's mother had tried to sell her the god because 48 didn't want it. Wu Chieh asked 369 why she thought 48 was ill. "Well, it is because of the $90 that her husband took and gave to a friend to go and gamble. It was 47 who took that money." Wu Chieh asked: "Is that true?" 369: "Sure, everyone saw this." 369 then told Wu Chieh that she and 447 (F 35) were standing earlier in the yard outside of 48's house wondering if she could sleep and 48 overheard them and yelled: "No. No. I am just going to throw myself up and down until I die."

Wu Chieh said that later, when she was doing child observations, she overheard 48's mother telling 48 that she had found the money in a drawer and asked her if she wanted to keep it herself or if she wanted "mother" to keep it for her. Later Wu Chieh heard 48 shouting: "I don't want to live here. I don't want to live here." 47 then said, "All right. As soon as you are well we will move away." Wu Chieh says that on Monday you could hear 48 banging things and laughing and yelling all the way across the yard on the main path. Wu Chieh heard her saying over and over, "Mother, I didn't want to do it, I didn't want to do it." Wu Chieh says that on the first day of her illness she kept calling for her mother, saying: "Mother, mother, I told you. I told you. I didn't want it that way."

Wu Chieh said that today there are three gods in 47's house: Wang Yeh, Wu Nien Ch'ing Swei, and Shang Ti Kung.

March 9, 1960

Yesterday when the *tang-ki* was called for 48 and told the family that 48 had been scared by a ghost, the god gave them three "*fu*" [magical charms] to call back 48's soul. One of them is to be burned at the Tu Ti Kung temple when they ask him to bring back 48's soul. Another one (or perhaps both of them) will be burned when they do the ritual to actually call back 48's soul. Wu Chieh says that 48 didn't answer her questions about this because she is not supposed to talk about what the god tells one. One should just do what the god tells one without questioning his instructions. Wu Chieh says that the god also told the family to *kho kun* tonight.*

Later in the day, 47 told Wu Chieh: "My mother-in-law just went home. She won't pay any attention to me. She won't do what I tell her to do. She says she is tired to death. How can I do all these things [referring to the rituals prescribed by

---

* Kho kun refers to making offerings of food, incense, and ritual money for all the local gods and their "troops."

the god, taking care of the children, watching out for 48, etc.]?" 128 (F 34), 487 (F 50), 439 (F 57) and a woman from Western Village were present when 47 said this. They all agreed with what 47 said and sympathized, saying it was too bad. 128: "You know, you have to do all these rituals before the sun goes down; you have to *bai-bai* before the sun goes down. And if you are going to *kho kun*, you have to cook now." 439 agreed: "Yes, and you have to *bai-bai* to Tu Ti Kung before the sun goes down. Did you do that yet?" 47: "I didn't do that yet. How can I get away to do that? 439 then said that she and the others would watch 48 while 47 went to *bai-bai* to Tu Ti Kung. As far as we know, no one in the village has volunteered to help 47 take care of 48 or the children or to cook for him. When 47 left to go *bai* to Tu Ti Kung, 48 called 49 (her son) into the house and lay on the bed with him. The women told Wu Chieh that she still likes her children very much even though she is sick, and that she wants 49 with her so that his father won't spank him. 47 is very mad at 49 because he told his mother that a medicine that 47 gave her was made of worms. This was a dose prescribed by the gods. 128: "This 47 really is stupid. People who want the god's help shouldn't tell other people about what the god said. 47 told people and was even in there asking his wife if she felt better yet. (You are not supposed to question what a god tells you, just do it and assume the result will be good.) If you keep on asking questions even a doctor will get mad and say why do you come here if you don't believe me?" Then 439 took 51 (48's two-year-old son) and put him next to his mother and pulled 49 out of his mother's arms, telling 48: "Why don't you take care of the little one instead of that big one?"

128 told everyone that she heard 48 questioning 49 about whether or not his father had given her worms in the medicine. Then 49 came out of the house looking scared and saying that his mother had run out. They went after her.

Later, 26 (F 45) told the women: "Yesterday 48 said that

she wanted the god who walked across the water and said that if she had the god she would be all right. She told them not to talk about the price and that she would ask when she got well." 26 was angry because 128 had said that 47 would scold her. 26 said: "I don't believe that he would scold me. 47 scolded 48's mother for having spent too much money on the god. That is why 48's mother went home." (48's mother carried 50 home on her back.) 26: "When her mother said that she would go get the god, 48 was all right and got up and put on her good clothes and high heels. But then when her mother returned with the god and 47 scolded her, 48 got sick again right away. This dumb 47. He doesn't understand what is important. She will never get well this way."

Later 395 (M 51) heard the children all crying in 48's bedroom and told 47 to go look after the children. He said, "Oh, it doesn't matter, it doesn't matter. It is all right now. It is just that her soul went away. It is all right now. The kids can stay with her at night."

30 (M 31) asked 47 if he had said anything to 48's mother. 47: "No, I just told her not to buy it, that's all. She just didn't want to help me. She just said that she was tired to death and went home. That's all. The god says that he will let her get well in five days. I don't know whether these things are true or not." 395 quickly said: "You mustn't say that. Don't say things like that. You must believe that she will get well." 47: "Well, if she doesn't get well by Saturday, I am going to send her to the hospital. I have already talked to my sister, and she says that it costs $180 a month." 395: "What hospital?" 47 hushed her with his hand over his mouth, and 395 said, "You are right, we shouldn't say."

(48's mother returned the next morning.)

March 10, 1960

This morning when Wu Chieh visited House 7, 48 was lying on the bed making *bai-bai* motions and saying, "I will

instruct everyone to do good things and not do bad things."
She lay flat on her back, moving her arms up and down as
though she were *bai-bai*-ing in a temple. "Because I have not
done any bad things, the god is always protecting me. If it
wasn't that the god was protecting me, I would have already
died in childbirth. From the time I was a child, everyone bullied me and I was unwilling to let them keep on doing this to
me, so I went and jumped into the river. The eighth god who
crossed the ocean, half of his body was in the water and half
was out, and that is why I was saved." (The village women
think this refers to Shang Ti Kung, and that it was Shang Ti
Kung who saved 48.) 48 repeated "I know, I know," over and
over again. Her mother asked her, like petitioning a *tang-ki*,
why her younger brother was out drinking all the time. 48:
"Don't you worry, Mother. He will get past this." Mother:
"What about your sister-in-law? We asked her for hardly anything when she married in, so why is she bullying me all the
time now?" 48: "Oh, this is two wrongs taking revenge on
one another. Don't get angry, Mother. When you get angry,
come to me and then you will be all right. This will all pass
too, slowly. Mother, you just stay with me for ten days and
cook for me because I can't cook anything now, then after
that you won't have to ever do anything again. But come to
me when you get angry, Mother, and then you will be all
right." (Wu Chieh says that sometimes 48 uses a Chinese
opera-style voice when she talks and sometimes she uses her
own voice.)

439 (F 57) came in and asked 48 if she knew who she was.
48 said that her heart was in confusion and she would have
to think for a minute. Then she jumped up and threw her
arms around 439, shouting, "Great prosperity." This made
439 very happy and she laughed excitedly. She turned to the
other women, "Did you hear that? Did you hear? I will have
great prosperity." Wu Chieh says she sincerely believed what
48 said to her.

Finally 48 told all the women to go home and go about their business. "I want to sleep now."

March 10, 1960

When Wu Chieh went back to House 7 this afternoon a group of 40 or 50 people were gathered in the house and the yard. They included 25 (M 49), 26 (F 45), 29 (F 15), 31 (F 30), 76 (F 34), 83 (F 64), 85 (F 32), 93 (F 58), 94 (M 31), 95 (F 30), 106 (F 25), 126 (M 78), 128 (F 34), 133 (F 45), 153 (F 54), 154 (F 31), 164 (F 27), 170 (F 38), 175 (M 31), 192 (F 27), 197 (F 35), 182 (F 33), 497 (F 30), 225 (F 35), 244 (F 70), 263 (F 56), 330 (M 59), 366 (F 43), 367 (F 15), 369 (F 24), 373 (F 41), 375 (F 24), 376 (F 19), 395 (M 51), 399 (F 15), 427 (F 47), 439 (F 57), 479 (F 37), 487 (F 50), 489 (F 26), 486 (M 27), 488 (M 18), the schoolmaster's mother-in-law, and a large number of people from Western Village.

439 (F 57), 366 (F 43), and 395 (M 51) were saying to each other and to Wu Chieh: It must be true that the god has come into her body because everything she says is right. The people were talking about how 48 sent her husband to buy a god at a particular place, and that she had said that the people shouldn't change Tzu Shih Yeh's birthday to the second of March because the new god (the one she had her husband buy) will have his eyes opened [the god will enter the image for the first time] on the second of March. She also said, "If people don't believe in this god, they will die. Everyone will die."

As the people present were discussing these things, 47, whom 48 had sent to a certain place to buy the image of the god, returned and said: "She was right. She was right. There is a god like that there, but they want $240 for it and I didn't have that much money." 182 (F 33) ran home to get some money and came back and slipped it into 47's pocket without saying anything. 128 (F 34) offered to give 47 $120 but he did not take it, saying that 182 had already given him the money. As soon as 47 returned, 48's mother told 48 that they had found the god but had to go back to bring it home because 47 didn't have enough money. As soon as she heard this, 48 jumped off the bed and began to *bai-bai* in the house and then in the yard. She would kneel down and *bai-bai* with her hands clasped together, her head shaking violently. Occasionally she would fall forward onto her hands and lie there for a minute before she got up and started all over again. From time to time she made the "counting motions" with her hands which is a traditional *tang-ki* gesture. All the time she was breathing very heavily. As soon as this happened, the women all told one another to stop talking and all began to watch very closely.

When 128 came up and offered the money to 47, she called out 128's name and then began to *bai-bai* with large gestures. When 128 started to move away, 48 motioned for her to stop and then said: "Oh, you loaned the money to me. Oh, you loaned the money to me." After a little, 128 again tried to leave, and 48 suddenly jumped up and pointed at 85 (F 32) and told her to approach. 85 had been chatting with some other women about some medicine that she had put on her eyes which appeared to be infected. She looked quite scared, and the others had to push her forward, saying, "Go on, see what she has to say." As soon as 85 reached her, 48 touched 85's eyes with her hand and said, "All right. This one will be well." She sounded as if she was reading a formal notice. 48 then went back to the *bai-bai* motions, saying to 85: "Your 84 is a good man. He has a kind heart. He took me home one night on his bicycle. Your family will have peace and won't have any trouble." 85 was holding her baby, who began to cry very loudly. 83 (F 64) came up and tried to remove 48's hands, telling her that the baby was crying because she had to urinate. 48 pushed 83's hands away and said in a loud commanding voice, "Never mind." She then began to handle the baby, saying, "You will have peace and you won't have any trouble. It doesn't matter. It doesn't matter." And then to 85 she said, "In these days everything will be all right. Everything will be all right." She made more *bai-bai* motions and then finally commanded 85 to go home and not to talk to anyone on the way. "Do you understand?" 85 was still smiling, but she was probably quite frightened for her face had turned white.

After 85 left, 48 knelt on the threshold and made *bai-bai* motions and said, "It is not me. It is not me. Anyone who has trouble, come to me in ten days, in ten days."

After doing more *bai-bai*, she suddenly called Wu Chieh's name. Wu Chieh was afraid and didn't want to go forward. She asked 439 what to do. 439 misunderstood her and thought Wu Chieh was asking what was wrong. "Nothing is wrong. The god is in her body, that's all." The crowd urged Wu Chieh to come forward, and 48's mother also told Wu Chieh to approach. 48 moved her hands over Wu Chieh's body and face and then took her hands and began to "jump" like a *tang-ki*. Some of the people in the crowd laughed and said, "She wants to dance with you, Wu Chieh." 48 said to Wu Chieh: "Older Sister, you come and are very kind to all of the children. From the top of the village to the bottom of the village, all of the children call you Older Sister. Do you like that? Do you like that?" Wu Chieh was speechless with fear. 48's mother told her to answer, and Wu Chieh managed to blurt out, "Yes." 48 hugged her very close and put her face against Wu Chieh's. Her mother said: "She wants to kiss you." 48 said, "No! No! No!" and her mother said quickly, "No, I am wrong. I am wrong. I am just an old lady who doesn't understand." 48 told the crowd through gestures, reaching in her pocket, smacking her lips, etc., that Wu Chieh gave the children candy. "Children, adults, and old people are all the same. You know that, right?" Wu Chieh agreed. 48 began to make wide sweeping *bai-bai* gestures, and said, "People should not be judgmental, saying this person is good and that person is bad." Then she began to "jump" again, and 94 (M 31) hissed at Wu Chieh, "Stupid child, aren't you going to run away?" Some little boys were giggling and saying, "This crazy lady is dancing, and poor Older Sister is going to have to wash all her clothes." (48 was dirty from kneeling and falling in the courtyard.) 48 turned on the boys and shouted, "Go away if you don't believe. Go away." She waved them off as if they were curious chickens, and they scattered like chickens. She turned again to Wu Chieh, rubbed her hands, telling her that everything would be peaceful with her.

As she talked, she continued to make *bai-bai* motions, to jump about, and finally fell over backward on the ground. She lay on the ground for some time, and Wu Chieh said that when she opened her eyelids, all she could see were the whites of her eyes. After a bit, she got up and told everyone to go away, saying: "If you don't and you meet something bad, don't blame me."

People moved off to the edge of the yard, some of them whispering, some of them laughing, but after a bit, the crowd slowly began to edge toward the house. 48 told Wu Chieh: "Because they bully me, I am not willing to continue. Do you understand? Do you? You must take me out. Do you understand that?" Wu Chieh kept saying, "Yes, yes" at the urging of 48's mother, but she wasn't at all sure what was expected of her. After a few more minutes, 48 told Wu Chieh to go home and not to talk with anyone she met on the way. She repeated her order to Wu Chieh and said, "Listen to what I say or it won't go well for me. After you go home, then come back and take me into the house." People were urging Wu Chieh to leave so she started to walk away, but 48 called her back one more time. "I haven't finished talking to you yet. If you don't listen to me, things will go bad for you. Do you understand? Now, hurry up and go home and then come back and take me into my room. Will you do that? If you don't, I will come to your house and find you." 48 repeated these instructions several times and added: "When you come back, if I am still talking to these women, you stand here and don't say anything. Do you hear me?" This was all said in a loud and commanding voice, totally unlike her normal voice. Finally 48's mother told her that Wu Chieh had said she would come back, and 48 grabbed both of Wu Chieh's hands in one of hers and gestured with her other hand in the "counting" motions of the *tang-ki* who is "calculating" what goes on in the world. (This is considered an indication of the god's omniscience.) 48 finally pushed Wu Chieh away and told her yet again to go home and not to speak with anyone on the way. Wu Chieh fled. Her husband was at home so she made him go back with her, and on the way several people told her that 48 was calling for her. When she got back to 48's house, 48 was on her hands and knees, with her head hanging. 48's mother urged Wu Chieh to tell 48 she was back and ready to take her into the house. She did so and after a while, 48 got to her feet and staggered after her into the house like she was drunk, feeling along the wall for the door to the bedroom. She kept right on doing *bai-bai* gestures, however. Wu Chieh led her to the bedroom and got her to lie down. She did, but without pausing in her gestures, counting, calculating, and doing *bai-bai*. Wu Chieh ran out.

Later in the day, Wu Chieh met 427 (F 47), who questioned her about the afternoon's events. 427: I wonder if the god is really pointing out a *tang-ki*?" Wu Chieh said she didn't know. 427: "When Ong Hue-lieng came and called back her soul, she grabbed him and almost knocked him down. Then she grabbed her husband and pulled him into the bedroom saying she wanted to 'be a bride with him.' If she was a real *tang-ki*, all she would be saying was the god's words and not things like this."

Tonight Wu Chieh heard 479 (F 37) and 487 (F 50) talking about the events of the day, and they agreed that she couldn't be a real *tang-ki* because she seemed to be talking aimlessly at times.

Wu Chieh said that many of the children in the village had watched 48 all afternoon and were quite frightened. They ran after Wu Chieh when she left and asked what 48 had said to her and asked whether or not she was frightened. They seemed to want her reassurance. 48's own children were also present and didn't seem to be frightened. They did rush to pick her up when she fell down a couple of times.

83 (F 64), 439 (F 57), 366 (F 43), 128 (F 34), 395 (M 51) seem to believe that 48 is a real *tang-ki*. Most of the other women are still doubtful. During the afternoon events reported above, only 84 (M 39) and 330 (M 59) among the people in the crowd we talked with doubted that a god was somehow involved.

March 14, 1960

Today the general attitude of the village towards 48 seems to be that she is crazy and not a *tang-ki*. 383 (F 32), 388 (F 27), 376 (F 19) all told Wu Chieh that they think 48 is just crazy. "If she were a real *tang-ki*, she wouldn't say she wanted to have 'the first night of marriage' with her husband. It isn't true that she is a *tang-ki*. She is just crazy. Last night she went over to 127's house and knelt on the threshold and accused him of stealing a hundred dollars from her. 127 (M 39) said: 'Oh what bad luck I have.' He was pretty mad before she left."

On the path to the school this morning, Wu Chieh overheard 124 (F 8) telling the other children, "Last night when she came in I was just getting ready to go to bed and my sister, 123 (F 11), was studying. 48 banged on the door, and 544 (F 16) had to keep asking her to go home. 544 was very scared and almost fainted when 48 wouldn't go home. 94 (M 31) came and told her to go home, but she still wouldn't go. When 11 (F 49) saw her coming, she quietly closed all the doors so she couldn't get in. She said that 121 (F 54) had stolen her money, and that 121 had borrowed NT$900 from her. How could this be? My grandmother says that she gave her back all her money. And how could she steal her money?"

March 14, 1960
Present: 31 (F 30), 113 (F 25), & 9 (F 84)

Wu Chieh asked: "Is 48 really a *tang-ki*?" At first they all answered "Who knows?" Wu Chieh: "Did you go see Ong Hue-lieng call back her soul?" 113 said she didn't because they had *fu* hanging up and "I am still a mother-within-the-month." Wu Chieh: "Where is the *fu*?" 113: "They have cloth hanging out in front of the house to call back her soul." (The *fu* is over the door.) Wu Chieh: "Oh, she told us that 85 (F 32) would be all well in three days." 113 and 31 both laughed and said, "That is not true. She is just crazy. If it was really true she wouldn't say that she wanted to be a bride with her husband. Ong Hue-lieng said that it wasn't true. He says that she is just crazy." 113: "Last night they had a doctor in and he gave her a shot and told them not to let people stand around and look at her. You have to believe in the gods, but you have to have a doctor to do something about it too. They just kept thinking that the god was in her body and kept asking the god for help and didn't give her any medicine. How could she get well this way?"

479 (F 37) also told Wu Chieh that it wasn't true that 48 was a *tang-ki*. 479: "Oh, Ong Hue-lieng is an old man who has been studying this kind of thing for a long time and can tell if it is a real one or not, and he says it isn't true. I don't think it's true either. Yesterday everyone was saying that it was true, and 26 (F 45) was telling everyone that when she was in the house, she smelled puffs of fragrant air. But that is not true."

Wu Chieh asked 121 (F 54) about 48 and she said: "Oh, I just have bad luck. I didn't get home from the south until last night, and the kids were scared to death. She just pushed into the house and said that I stole her $90. She said that when she was going down to the river I told her not to lock the door and then went in and stole her money. I just have bad luck."

83 (F 64), 85 (F 32), 106 (F 25). When Wu Chieh questioned them about 48 they said they didn't know, but later they said that Ong Hue-lieng knew about these things and he said that it isn't true. "She is just crazy." Wu Chieh: "Why doesn't she like 492 (F 28) and 140 (F 39)? When did they have trouble?" 106: "She was going to 492's home, and 492 closed the doors. 85: "492 says that it was the children who closed the doors. Then 48 got mad and picked up a stick and banged on the door. You see these two haven't talked to one another for a long time because of their children fighting." Wu Chieh: "Why is she mad at 140 then?" "Oh, they were okay at first, but then they had an argument so that now they don't talk to one another. 140 got mad because 47 went to tell her husband something about her. Yesterday 48 went over to 140's house, and 140 hid in the kitchen. But 48 stood in the yard *bai-bai*-ing, and when 140 stuck her head out, 48 called her and she had to come out. As soon as 140 came out, 48 said: '140, 140, are you mad at me? Are you mad at me?' 140 said she wasn't mad at her. 48 insisted that she call her by name, so 140 called her name several times and then said she wasn't mad at her. 48 knelt down to *bai-bai*, saying: '140, I am sorry. I am sorry. I am coming to redress a grievance for 47. 47 is just stubborn. I say I am sorry to you for him. I say I am sorry to you in his place.'"

83: "Today she heard that 173 (M 66) wasn't feeling good, and so she wanted him to come and let her cure him." Others: "Did he go?" 83: "Yes, and she just did the same thing and rubbed him on the chest and told him to go home and he would be all right." Wu Chieh: "I heard that 26 was telling everyone that she smelled fragrant air in the house." 83: "This is true. I smelled it too." Wu Chieh: "What does it mean?" 83: "This means that the god is there. It is very hard to be sure about this. A lot of things she said were right, and all of the things she said were good things. She may be crazy, but she can remember who was good to her and who was bad to her." 85: "Yes, but I asked 84 about this last night, and he couldn't remember that he had done that for her. That Ong Hue-lieng is a good man. When he heard about all this, he came to see whether it was a god or not. He just came and told 48's mother that he would do all of this for her. No one asked him to come. He understands all of these things and knows how to tell."

Wu Chieh overheard 121 (F 54) telling 83 about 48's accusing her of stealing her money. 83: "Yes, we know she is crazy and if you get hit by her then there is nothing you can do." 121: "47 kept telling me to look at his face and not argue with her. So I told 48 that if I had taken her money, I would be more sick than she is, and none of the people in my family would prosper. I vowed that I didn't take her money. Boy, what bad luck I have." 89 (F 32): "Oh, she has been saying that someone stole her money ever since she went crazy. But that was the right thing for you to do."

324 (F 39) to Wu Chieh: "128 (F 34) was telling me that that *ti ki* [silly] man 94 (M 31) got scared. Remember what she said to you when she grabbed you? Well, 128 told me that last night 94 was standing there smoking, and 48 came and grabbed him and told him to go home. Then she said: 'You are a very good person. You are a very good person. But I am being sarcastic, you know that, don't you?' 94's face was all red and he was sweating. Then she grabbed him and rubbed his chest and told him not to be scared. 'If you want to say that it is not true, you may, but it is half true.' Last night they gave her a shot and said they didn't want anyone to visit her because she gets upset when people are around."

388 (F 27), 383 (F 32), and 402 (F 26) were discussing 48 and the different reasons that might account for her illness. 388: "Maybe it really is because she lost that hundred dollars. She found it now, so she's all right again." 402: "Maybe it really was that god. But I don't think so. I think that it was

because she was crazy once before. People who have this kind of sickness once always get it again." 383: "Yes, like old Wu. When he was all right, he could run the business and everything, but when he was sick he didn't know anything. They would take him to a doctor and he would be all right for a while but then later he would get it again. I think that maybe she is the same." 383: "Once when we were living in Tamsui, there was a young man who was very earnest and filial. He was going to marry a girl, but she ran away on the day of the engagement, so the girl's mother told the boy's mother that she would give the boy money if he would wait and marry her later. The boy's mother wouldn't let him marry anyone else because she knew the girl's mother would give her daughter lots of money when she married into the family. Later the boy did marry this girl. The first time I saw her, her eyes looked different from other people's eyes, and then a few months after they got married, she got sick and didn't know anything. That mother, just because she wanted the girl's money, she got that kind of a daughter-in-law, and the poor man . . . He was a very good man, and he got that kind of wife."

March 15, 1960

330 (M 59) told Wu Chieh that the god that 48 bought has a face that is half white and half black. 330: "She is too dumb. Just because of a hundred dollars she gets all this. She is just too dumb."

366 (F 43) and 106 (F 25) told Wu Chieh that 48 is *bai-bai*-ing again today and saying that today is the birthday of the god she bought. She is going to make "the five kinds of food" for the god's birthday. She also wanted to make 60 turtles [ceremonial cakelike offerings made in the shape of turtles] and give one to every family in the village, but 153 (F 54) talked her out of this, saying that the family did not have enough money, so she is only going to make 12 turtles. 93 (F 58) went to see her this morning, and she hid her face in

her hands when she saw 93, and finally she ran back into the kitchen and knelt in a corner and hid her face in her hands.

11 (F 49), 4 (F 28), 590 (F 26), & 487 (F 50). This morning 47 came to ask 10 [11's husband and the clerk for the district] for a certificate of some sort that he would need to send 48 to the mental hospital, and 10 told him that he would have to get this from the county government office in Pan Ch'iao. 487: "I thought that the reason she got sick is just because she lost the money and worried about it. As soon as she found the money, she felt better. Besides this, 121 swore in her house in front of the god that she hadn't stolen the money." 4: "Oh, I think that it was just because of her health. If her mind was really sick, she wouldn't have been able to get well so fast." 487: "Maybe that's right, because before she got sick she often told her husband that her heart felt as though there was a fire burning in it."

March 15, 1960

154 (F 31) to Wu Chieh: "Very early this morning 48 came here and told my mother that she wanted to *bai-bai* to that god today and make 60 turtles and give one to every family in the village. She said that today the god is going to open his mouth and say something so that everyone in the village will believe in him. My mother told her that she had already spent a lot of money and that she wasn't rich and that her husband wasn't working now, so why didn't she just use a little pork and a little fish and make 12 turtles and then have a big *bai-bai* when the family has more money. So finally 48 went to her mother with the money to buy the things. She ran over here when she heard that her husband was going to send her to that hospital, but her mother called her back. Her mind is getting clearer now. 128 (F 34) went to see her, and 48 told her that there was nothing wrong with her. She said, 'They just sent me to the hospital and tied up my hands and legs and left me there for two days, and they charged us NT$400.

You know that money wasn't easy to earn.' She kept saying that 47 is too dumb. I asked 128 why she said this, and she said she thought it was because 47 wouldn't believe in the god. 48 said: 'You are too dumb, so why not just get divorced. I am a woman and you are a man, so I'll take the one girl and you take the boys. I won't have to take your boys. I'm going to take the girl home with me. I am going to take my girl home with me.' That is why she has the girl 50 with her every time she runs away. Like this last time, she had 50 on her back." Wu Chieh: "Did someone tell her that 47 was going to take her to the hospital?" 154: "No. I didn't even know until her mother told me. I don't know how she found out about it."

March 16, 1960

Wu Chieh asked 366 (F 43) if 48's family really found the money that 48 lost, or if they just gave her some money. 366: "I don't know for sure, but I think they really found it because as soon as 121 (F 54) swore before the god that she hadn't taken it and said that she would get sick herself if she had, 439 (F 57) found the money in the bottom of a drawer in the pocket of some old clothes. Then 48's mother burned incense and asked the god to take care of 48 and 121, and not let anything happen to them. So it must be that they really found the money."

170 (F 38) told Wu Chieh that yesterday 48's younger sister 52 came back and gave 48 $500 because she knew that it was because of money that 48 had gotten sick. 48's mother also gave her $300. 170: "So now with this money and the money they found, she has almost a thousand dollars. 48 has been scolding 47 because he won't go to work."

There is some possibility that the god that 48 is *bai-bai*-ing to is a god of her own creation, which would be interesting if true because it might be an example of how new gods appear in the Taiwanese religious scene. This is not a god from 48's home in Keelung because her mother had never heard of the god. The people here now only know of this name as a group name from the eight immortals. The store where the god was bought did not have such a god and had to paint it to order on another figure. Furthermore, 48's mother did not know when the god's birthday should be. 128 (F 34) told Wu Chieh that when they *bai-bai*-ed to the god today, 48's mother said: "We don't know when you were born, so we will *bai-bai* to you today and then every year on this day. 128: "And then 48's mother used the *poe-a* to ask the god if this was all right,* and the god said no four times. 48 saw this and she asked the god, and the god answered yes on the first try. So it must be that only 48 herself knows about this god."

Wu Chieh asked 262 (M 63): "Do you think the god really came into 48's body?" 262 laughed and suggested that Wu Chieh go ask 48. Wu Chieh: "I heard that if a person does something wrong, the god would punish them. Is this true?" 262: "Sure." Wu Chieh: "How would the god punish?" 262: "The god will make you sick." Wu Chieh: "I have heard that the god will kill people with lightning." 262: "Yes, that is right, but you have to have done something really bad." Wu Chieh: "Has this ever happened around here?" 262: "Yes. 445's husband's older brother was killed by lightning. He always seemed to be a very good man, but he must have done something that no one knew about."

* *Poe-a* are half-moon-shaped blocks of wood that, when dropped, reveal the god's answer of yes, no, or "laughing" by the way they fall.

Commentary

To my eye, the material above looks very unlike the G (for general) data cards from which it was copied. The G data are grubby 5 × 8 cards, splattered in places with the juicier parts of insects. This particular set of notes differs from the nearly 1,200 such cards of "miscellaneous data" collected during a long stretch of fieldwork in Taiwan between 1958 and 1961, in that more of it comes directly from one of our field assistants. Wu Chieh was so engaged by these events that she more or less went on strike from her normal duties until the drama subsided. Since we were very much involved in another aspect of our research at that point, Wu Chieh exercised considerably more independence than usual. She kept us informed of village opinion and goings-on, but she often chose for herself what people to interview about Mrs. Tan and, I suspect, which of her conversations she would report. Nonetheless, even those data she collected of her own volition show something of the perspective of the anthropologist. She had been trained by us to ask certain kinds of questions and take note of certain kinds of behaviors. She is quite intelligent and learned this lesson well. I don't doubt that it influenced what she saw and how she described it to us.

Still, ever since I began this project I have wondered about the extent to which Wu Chieh lived a double life during this time, reporting one set of interviews and observations for the foreign anthropologists and collecting another set for herself, an unsophisticated nineteen-year-old Taiwanese woman who was trying to make sense out of her own world. There were times during the years we lived and worked together that Wu Chieh and I talked a lot about "life." Unfortunately, this was not one of those times, and nothing in my personal journal tells me what, if anything, she was thinking about the Tan

*

affair other than what she reported to us and I recorded in the fieldnotes. As much as (if not more than) any other voice in the village, Wu Chieh's unexpurgated reflections on what she saw, heard, and thought she understood to be happening would have provided interesting insights into the events. I now realize it would also have been very interesting methodologically: it would have given us some understanding of the filter through which we received much of the data on which *our* understanding was based. But, then, it would also have been interesting to know the various influences on and biases of *each* of our "important" informants in Peihotien. We cannot, and that, of course, is one reason why our truths will always be partial at best (Clifford 1986).

But Wu Chieh certainly did have a major influence on us when she chose the topic that *she* thought we should be attending to and pulled us into it, willy-nilly. This is, apparently, not an unusual situation for anthropologists. Renato Rosaldo, in an account that has now become classic, describes how he spent long, mind-numbing evenings writing down endless lists of place-names that brought tears to the eyes of his informants but left him "in uncomprehending boredom" (1980: 16). Only after he had left the field did he recognize the significance of what his informants had insisted that he record. They had taught him not just their history, but their historiography as well, the way in which they thought about their past.

The fieldnotes I present in this chapter are by no means central to an understanding of Chinese patterns of thought, but they have been a critical aid to me in my attempt to distinguish some thirty years later between two realities, one as observed and recorded by our field staff, and another consciously constructed by me. Perhaps because it has a beginning and a middle and an end, the fiction I created ("The Hot Spell") seemed to me when I came upon it again after all these years to be an accurate rendering of what had happened— except, of course, for the flash flood. But when I went back to the fieldnotes, to my diaries, and to letters written to family and friends in the United States during that time, a different version began to emerge. Without these notes, I would have had no check on the account in the short story.

But what, in fact, are fieldnotes? Unvarnished descriptions of events as they occur? Unanalyzed facts gathered from participants in the event? Are they the essential link between behavior on the ground and the ethnography on the shelf? For all anthropologists? Roger Sanjek brought together a group of people at the 1985 meetings of the American Anthropological Association to discuss these topics and eventually collected their papers (along with some important additions of his own) in *Fieldnotes: The Makings of Anthropology* (1990). Attitudes toward fieldnotes differ greatly, according to Jean Jackson, who talked with seventy anthropologists before writing her contribution to the Sanjek volume. Some hold their notes in a reverence that embarrasses even them (Jackson 1990: 27–28; Ottenberg 1990: 141); some read and reread them (Wolf 1990b: 347ff); some vow they barely look at them when they write their ethnographies (Jackson 1990: 11; Plath 1990: 372). But in one way or another, all anthropologists seem to make some kinds of notes in the process of fieldwork that end up having some kind of effect on their later writing. Whether they are of the simple description type or a running-conversation-with-oneself type, they come home under special cover and occupy a special (if not always honored) place in the anthropologist's study. They are the first sacred text in the preparation of ethnography.

The word text rears its head again. A glance at any paragraph in the fieldnotes will convince the reader that they are a text, and that the information in it is only a partial description of an activity, a conversation, a scene. It cannot be otherwise, for the action is frozen, and so few words cannot capture all the activity that occurs in a few minutes of observation and the social and material context that gives that activity meaning. As such, it is fair to say that fieldnotes are the first summary of behavior, the initial endowment of it with significance. The construction of a partial and incomplete version of a reality observed by the anthropologist begins with the writing of fieldnotes. For several of the contributors to the Sanjek collection, these are sufficient reasons to distrust one's notes.

Other anthropologists look at their fieldnotes with misgivings because in time these notes come to be in disagreement with what Simon Ottenberg (1990: 144) has aptly labeled "headnotes." Both headnotes and fieldnotes are created in the fieldwork setting, but fieldnotes do not change once they are written down. Headnotes, even while in the field, are constantly being revised as new material is discovered, more experiences are processed, early hunches prove false. When the head returns home, it continues to revise and elaborate the headnotes as it encounters new theories, comparative data, and internal inconsistencies. But the anthropologist does not alter the fieldnotes.

Ottenberg states that ethnography is the product of both fieldnotes and headnotes, but he considers his headnotes more important (1990: 147). I do not see my fieldnotes as "sacred," but I do see them as an essential corrective to my memory, which has been known to shift an opinion from the mouth of a male elder to that of his feisty young daughter-in-law, and to attach a set of brothers to the wrong lineage simply because they seemed to spend more time with members of that lineage. Headnotes are too easy to revise to suit some current theory, but even flawed fieldnotes have to be dealt with on their original terms. Reinterpreted, yes; revised, no. The errors in my fieldnotes and in my diaries remain there to humble me each time I read them; my "headnotes" are kinder—and more dangerous.

"The Hot Spell" is an excellent example of the hazards of relying on headnotes. The short story became a headnote for me, and one that was so vivid that it erased the version recorded in the fieldnotes. Except, of course, for the flash flood (one had occurred in the area but before our time and with no loss of life), what happened in the short story was the way it happened, according to my headnotes. According to my fieldnotes, many of the conversations and some of the action in "The Hot Spell" never happened. It is quite possible that some of those events did occur, were not recorded in the fieldnotes, and gradually faded from, or were slowly transformed, in my headnotes to fit the text of the short story.

So why did that account seem more vivid than other headnotes or the events as described in the fieldnotes? My guess is that unlike the fieldnotes or the events themselves, the short story brought closure. I was driven to write the story while still in the field because Mrs. Tan's actions troubled me, her fate was unclear, and her ignominious departure from the village turned the whole affair into a non-event. Wu Chieh had caught me up in the unfolding of a drama, and I needed a denouement. Perhaps I was not yet thinking like an anthropologist who is prepared to find the denouement in something like the essay in the next chapter. I certainly was not thinking like a postmodernist, who would be quite content with loose ends and unexplained aftershocks. I wonder how many "normal" (i.e., nonintellectual) humans are comfortable with the instability, ambiguity, ambivalence, and contradiction that delight postmodernists? Even that most intellectual of anthropologists, Clifford Geertz, asserts: "The claim to attention of an ethnographic account does not rest on its author's ability to capture primitive facts in faraway places and carry them home like a mask or a carving, but on the degree to which he is able to clarify what goes on in such places, to reduce the puzzlement—what manner of men are these?" (1973: 16). I concur, and I suspect that "reducing the puzzlement" had a lot to do with my unconscious suppression of the "facts" in the fieldnotes in favor of the "fiction" in the short story.

Ottenberg (who, remember, prefers his headnotes) claims, "My headnotes and my written notes are in constant dialogue" (1990: 146), but at least some others see fieldnotes as an essential corrective. For example, Rena Lederman says of hers:

> Fieldnotes are *dangerous*. Observations are noted or written down in order to aid memory, but reading fieldnotes can challenge memory. It threatens to return one to uncertainty about what was what; it acts against the sense of the whole that one carries around in one's head. Fieldnotes can contradict the single, anthropological voice we are all encouraged to adopt in our formal ethnographic writing at home by recording—however indirectly—the voices of the people we lived with when doing fieldwork. (1990: 73)

It is this tendency of anthropologists (humans?)—this incurable tendency to tell ourselves satisfying stories ("the sense of the whole that one carries around in one's head") to explain the perhaps unexplainable—that makes fieldwork and fieldnotes essential. Even the flawed methods of ethnography-building serve to remind us of how long the blank spans are that bridge the piers of what we know.

The fieldnotes in this chapter are not reflexive; nor, I suppose, could they be labeled dialogic.* The creator of the notes—whichever member of the field team that might be—is not always in them, but if read closely, the debate going on in the village, the disagreements over the cause of Mrs. Tan's behavior, the shifting of opinions, can be pieced together. Obviously, these entries are filtered through minds that had opinions, but my recollections and my personal journals suggest that at least this member of the field team was not pushing for a particular outcome. Still, there are clearly some assumptions. For example, I did not entertain the presence of a god as one of the explanations of Mrs. Tan's behavior, and I may have edited out of Wu Chieh's dictations to me hints of her own attitudes. Again, I regret that I did not reflect more at the time on Wu Chieh's unusual absorption in these incidents.

---

*The reader who notices a certain diffidence when I use the term dialogic will find me in good company. Paul Rabinow also (1986: 245–66) takes Clifford to task for his inconsistent use of the term.

My personal journals are rife with reflexivity, but on this incident they reveal only my own mystification about Mrs. Tan's behavior, my irritation with a research assistant who suddenly had become willful and irresponsible, and my dismay at my irritation.

Unless one has "been there," reading undoctored fieldnotes is not very interesting. There is no beginning, middle, or end, and nothing gets settled, let alone finished. Moreover, someone else's fieldnotes are devoid of the contextual materials, the ordering, that makes them comprehensible, and the sensory detail that makes their topic manifest. Nancy Lutkehaus (1990) describes her first two readings of Camilla Wedgwood's fieldnotes from Manam, a small island off Papua New Guinea, as having quite different effects on her. The first reading, just before she went to Manam, was very useful in providing information that allowed her to readily win the confidence of people who had known Wedgwood, but she found herself more interested in the author of the notes than in their content. After Lutkehaus had been in the field for a year, she took a break in Australia and again read through Wedgwood's papers. She comments:

Reading Wedgwood's notes was an entirely different experience the second time, for I was now reading the notes with the interest and knowledge of an insider. The people and activities she was describing were now "local history" for me, a chronicle of past events some of which I had heard about in other contexts, others of which illuminated present events. They filled in missing gaps in my understanding of the reasons why certain things happened or were done in a particular way. Details about people, places, terms, and events had an importance and relevance for me that they could not have had before I had actually been in the field and spent time living with the Manam, studying their culture, and getting to know individuals among them. (1990: 315)

To make use of Wedgwood's notes (and Lutkehaus goes on to describe a similar problem Wedgwood herself had with the notes of a yet earlier researcher), Lutkehaus had to recreate the context that Wedgwood had in her mind when she wrote them. Even though fifty years had passed, spending a year on Manam gave Lutkehaus that context. If we as anthropologists really "create" the cultures of which we write, how is it that these two women who never knew each other, who came from different social classes and different cultures, who were burdened with different theoretical approaches, and whose visits to Manam were separated by fifty years created much the same culture?*

But this is taking me away from the topic of fieldnotes and into the topic of the Commentary on the next chapter. I have included these unedited pages from our fieldnotes with all their problems of interpretation and internal inconsistency as an example of a stage in the anthropologist's attempt to explain one culture to members of another. Fieldnotes are bits and pieces of information filtered through the minds of those who observe and record them. Those tidbits of conversation, snippets of observation, and summaries of behavior that make it into the field record are highly selected from all that an anthropologist encounters in day-to-day life in (our case) a village. They cannot be pure descriptions of reality, no matter who collects them or writes them down. Even if observed and recorded by a villager, they would report a perspective that would outrage at least some other villagers. The fact that we choose to write down a particular piece of information implicates it in the beginning of an analysis. Our fieldnotes are the first ordering of "what we know."

Because, as I admitted earlier, these data were not collected in a period when we were being reflexive about our selves and our discipline, and these fieldnotes are not a verbatim dia-

---

*Mac Marshall (1989) raises this same question and answers it with some convincing examples from Japanese, German, and American anthropologists who knew little or nothing about each other's research. Robert J. Smith (1990: 364) speaks to the same issue in describing the remarkable work he and Ella Lury Wiswell crafted from her 1935–36 Suye Mura field journals (Smith & Wiswell 1982).

logue between anthropologists and informants that would allow the reader to judge why the researchers elicited the information they did, these notes have less to tell about the nature
of fieldwork than about the shreds and patches from which
a cultural description is constructed. In other words, these
unedited data, unlike the writings of a Jean-Paul Dumont
(1978), Kevin Dwyer (1982), or Paul Rabinow (1977), are
not included for their insights into field methodology but
rather to allow the patient reader to explore the way in which
one ethnographer develops contradictory opinions and confusing observations into clear and authoritative texts. There
is no final truth. Arthur Wolf does not dispute the events described in these fieldnotes—indeed, he recorded many of the
observations—but, he tells me, he has a different take on why
what happened happened. This is not surprising, for we are
very different anthropologists.

CHAPTER FOUR

The Woman Who Didn't Become a Shaman

IN THE SPRING of 1960, in a then remote village on the edge of the Taipei basin in northern Taiwan, a young mother of three lurched out of her home, crossed a village path, and stumbled wildly across a muddy rice paddy. The cries of her children and her own agonized shouts quickly drew an excited crowd out of what had seemed an empty village. Thus began nearly a month of uproar and agitation as this small community resolved the issue of whether one of their residents was being possessed by a god or suffering from a mental illness. For Mrs. Tan, it was a month of misery and exultation; for the residents of Peihotien, it was a month of gossip, uncertainty, and heightened religious interest; for the anthropologists in the village, it was a month of confusion and fascination.

Mrs. Tan herself had less influence over the outcome of her month of trial than a foreign observer might expect. Even Ong Hue-lieng, a religious specialist who lived nearby and who was given credit for making the final decision, was only one factor in a complex equation of cultural, social, ritual, and historical forces. In the pages that follow, I will attempt

© Reprinted from *American Ethnologist*, vol. 17, no. 3. © American Anthropological Association 1990. Personal names have been changed to match those used in the rest of the book; other minor changes were made to conform to Stanford University Press style.

to reconstruct the events of that spring from fieldnotes, journal entries, and personal recollections, and to evaluate what happened from the perspective of the anthropologist. I am concerned here not with shamanism per se, but with the social and cultural factors that were brought to bear by various members of the community in deciding whether Mrs. Tan was being approached by a god who wished to use her to communicate with his devotees, whether an emotional pathology included fantasies of spirit possession, or whether, as a few maintained, her feckless husband hoped to use her as a source of income.

In the hours following Mrs. Tan's precipitous trip into the mud of the rice paddies, an enormous amount of information traveled through the village about her recent behavior, her past, and the attitude of her family and neighbors. The day before, she had taken her six-month-old baby to her sister's house and left her. She had been complaining to her husband that there was a fever in her heart. She had beaten herself on the chest, pleading to be left in peace, and she had jumped up and down on the bed so violently that it had broken. Her husband, commonly referred to in the village as Dumb Tien-lai, had told one of their neighbors that she was probably going crazy "again." Nonetheless, he had done nothing about it until her very public display. Informants who were in the crowd that gathered as neighbors pulled her out of the paddy and took her back to her house reported that she begged to be allowed to go to the river to "meet someone" who was calling her. The nearby river is considered a dangerous place, full of the ghosts of people who have drowned there, in accidents or as suicides. Water ghosts are infamous for trying to pull in the living to take their place in the dark world of unhappy ghosts.

As the long afternoon wore on, we heard other reports. People said that she pleaded with her husband, Tan Tien-lai, to give her incense so that she could apologize to "the god who crossed the water." When he lit the incense for her, she began to tremble all over, her eyes glazed, and she began to talk in a loud male voice. One of the oldest women in the village, a woman known for her religious knowledge, came to see her and told Tien-lai that he should call in a *tang-ki* to see if she had met a ghost. By then, however, Mrs. Tan's husband had finally taken some action on his own, and the ranting woman was hauled off under some kind of restraint in a pedi-cab to what was described to me as a "mental hospital" in the nearby market town.

During the three days that Mrs. Tan was out of the village, the Tan family was part of every conversation. Arthur Wolf, our assistant Wu Chieh, and I collected information about the Tans whether we wanted it or not. We discovered that even though the family was extremely poor, Mrs. Tan went regularly to the temple in Tapu and visited others within walking dis-tance. Whenever her children were ill, she consulted *tang-ki* in Tapu and neighboring areas. At home, she burned incense and made offerings daily to both her husband's ancestors and a variety of spirits and gods. We learned that although she was painfully shy (we had had much less contact with her than with most other villagers), Mrs. Tan was a fiercely pro-tective mother who had quarreled in recent months with a woman from the Lim household when her young son had been slugged by a Lim boy. The Tans had lived in the village for nearly ten years, but by village tradition they were still newcomers—it took at least a generation for a new family to be accepted among those whose grandparents and great-grandparents had been born in Peihotien. Until then, new-comers were expected to behave like guests, and guests were expected to look carefully at their hosts' faces. It was a Lim village.

When Mrs. Tan returned to the village, pale and drugged, her mother, Mrs. Pai, had been called in by Tan Tien-lai to "help out." Mrs. Pai had none of her daughter's shyness, and the villagers soon learned from her that her daughter had had one previous "episode" of this kind of behavior. When she was a young adolescent, the family had come upon hard times and had been forced to give her away "in adoption" to a family in need of a servant. The girl had done fairly well until "something happened" about which the mother was vague in detail but implied that a member of the family had either raped or attempted to rape her. The girl had run away to her mother, been returned to her adoptive family, and within a few weeks been sent back to her parents by the adoptive family because "she was crazy." She stayed with her natal family until her marriage. There had been, according to her mother, no recurrence of erratic behavior.

Mrs. Pai also cast a new light on what might have precipitated her daughter's current distress. It seems that a couple of weeks earlier, a sizable sum of money had been lost from the pocket of her jacket. Mrs. Tan's son said he saw his father take it before he went out to gamble one night, but Tan Tien-lai denied it. Mrs. Tan blamed herself for the loss, but at times seemed convinced that it had been stolen by someone from the Lim household. At some point in the days that followed, the money was miraculously found (probably supplied by sympathetic villagers), but the expectation that this would end the problem was disappointed.

Within forty-eight hours of her return to Peihotien, Mrs. Tan was again drawing crowds. First she told her mother that she must *bai-bai* (worship) to "the god who crossed the ocean," a god unknown to Mrs. Pai. The old woman I mentioned earlier informed Mrs. Pai that this was probably Shang Ti Kung (a local god), and that it cost only one New Taiwan dollar (a few cents) per day to rent an image. She also urged her to bring in Shang Ti Kung's *tang-ki* to ask what was wanted. All of this was done the next day and, according to a neighbor, the *tang-ki* said that Mrs. Tan had met a ghost. Later that afternoon, the image of another god, Wang Yeh, was brought in, but Mrs. Tan was still not at peace. The next day, Mrs. Tan, according to her husband, leapt out of bed shouting that the god was in her body, and that Tien-lai must go at once to get the god's image so that she could *bai-bai* to him. They tried to humor her and finally, because she was getting more and more frantic, agreed to purchase the image. However, neither Tan Tien-lai nor his mother-in-law recognized the god she described. As Tan was discussing this problem with some neighbors, his mother-in-law came out of her daughter's bedroom and announced that the daughter, using a strange voice, had told her the exact place to purchase the god's image. She sent her son-in-law on his way, and, according to my informants, Mrs. Tan calmed down and went to sleep as soon as she heard that he had gone to purchase "the right god."*

Once the new god was put on the Tan household altar, however, the activities in the Tan courtyard changed dramatically. Mrs. Tan began to "dance" like a *tang-ki*, speak in a strange language, and make oracle-like statements. For nearly a week, whenever she came out of the house, crowds would gather and she would "perform." We did not attend all of her sessions, but we were told that she revealed knowledge about people's personal lives that "only a god could know." She behaved and spoke in ways that were most uncharacteristic of the withdrawn, depressed woman the village was accustomed to.

One session that our research assistant was involved in is a good example. I quote from our (slightly edited) fieldnotes:

Mrs. Tan suddenly jumped up and pointed at Lim Mei-ling and told her to approach. Lim Mei-ling had been chatting with some other women about some medicine she had put on her eyes, which appeared to be infected. She looked quite scared, and the others had to push her forward toward Mrs. Tan, saying, "Go on, see what she has to say." As soon as Lim Mei-ling reached her, Mrs. Tan touched Mei-ling's eyes and said, "All right. This one will be well." She sounded as if she were reading a formal notice. Mrs. Tan then returned to making *bai-bai* motions with her hands, saying: "Your

---

*We never did get a name for this god who needed a special paint job (with half his face black and half white) but still looked and acted very much like Shang Ti Kung to some of the people in the village who knew about such things.

husband is a good man. He has a kind heart. He took me home one night on his bicycle. Your family will have peace and won't have any troubles." Lim Mei-ling was holding her baby, who began to cry very loudly. Her mother-in-law came up and tried to take Mrs. Tan's hands off of Mei-ling, telling her that the baby was crying because she had to urinate. Mrs. Tan pushed her aside and said in a loud commanding voice, "Never mind." She then began to handle the baby, saying, "You will have peace and you won't have any trouble. It doesn't matter. It doesn't matter." To Mei-ling she said, "In these days everything will be all right for you. Everything will be all right." She made more *bai-bai* motions and then told Mei-ling to go home and not speak with anyone on the way. "Do you understand?" Mei-ling was still smiling, but she was probably quite frightened for her face had turned white. Mei-ling left and Mrs. Tan knelt on the threshold, making more *bai-bai* motions. She called our assistant, Wu Chieh, to come to her.

Wu Chieh was frightened and didn't want to go forward. She asked another woman what to do and was urged to comply. She was told, "Nothing is wrong. The god is in her body, that's all." Several people pushed Wu Chieh, including Mrs. Pai, Mrs. Tan's mother. Mrs. Tan moved her hands over Wu Chieh's body and face and then took her hands and began to "jump" like a *tang-ki.* Some of the people in the crowd laughed and said, "She wants to dance with you, Wu Chieh." Mrs. Tan said, "Older Sister, you come and you are very kind to all of the children. From the top of the village to the bottom, all of the children call you Older Sister. Do you like that? Do you like that?" Wu Chieh was speechless with fear. Mrs. Tan's mother told her to say something, and Wu Chieh blurted out, "Yes." Mrs. Tan hugged her close and put her face against Wu Chieh's. Mrs. Pai said, "She wants to kiss you." Mrs. Tan shouted, "No, no, no!" Her mother quickly said, "No, I am wrong. I am just an old lady who doesn't understand."

Mrs. Tan told the crowd through gestures (reaching in her pocket, smacking her lips, and so forth) that Wu Chieh gives the children candy. "Children, adults, and old people are all the same. You know that, right?" Wu Chieh nodded. Mrs. Tan then began to make wide, sweeping *bai-bai* gestures and pronounced, "People should not be judgmental, saying this person is good and that person is bad." Then she began to jump around the yard and an older woman hissed at Wu Chieh, "Stupid child, aren't you going to run away now?" Some little boys were giggling and saying, "This crazy lady is dancing and poor Wu Chieh is going to have to wash all of her clothes." (Mrs. Tan was dirty from kneeling and falling in the dusty courtyard.) Mrs. Tan immediately turned on the boys and shouted, "Go away if you don't believe. Go away." She waved them off as if they were curious chickens, and they scattered like chickens. She turned again to Wu Chieh and rubbed her hands, telling her that everything would be peaceful with her.

As she talked, she continued to make *bai-bai* motions, to jump about, and finally fell over backward on the ground. She lay there for some time and Wu Chieh said when Mrs. Tan opened her eyes, only the whites were visible. After a bit, Mrs. Tan got up and told everyone to go away, saying, "If you don't and you meet something bad [by implication, a ghost], don't blame me." People moved off to the edge of the yard, some of them whispering, some of them laughing, but after a bit the crowd slowly began to edge back toward the house. Mrs. Tan told Wu Chieh, "Because they bully me, I am not willing to continue. Do you understand? You must take me out. Do you understand that?" Wu Chieh kept agreeing at the urging of Mrs. Tan's mother but she wasn't at all sure of what was expected of her.

Mrs. Tan told Wu Chieh to go home again and not to talk with anyone she met on the way. "Listen to what I say or it won't go well for me. After you go home, then come back and take me into the house." People urged Wu Chieh to leave then, so she started to walk away, but Mrs. Tan called her back one more time. "I haven't finished talking to you yet," she said. "If you don't listen to me things will go bad for you. Do you understand? Now, hurry up and go home and then come back and take me to my room. Will you do that? If you don't, I will come to your house and find you." She repeated these instructions several times and added, "When you come back, if I am still talking to these women, you stand here and don't say anything, do you hear?" This was all said in a loud commanding voice, totally unlike her normal voice, according to Wu Chieh. Mrs. Tan grabbed both of Wu Chieh's hands in one of hers and gestured with the other in the "counting" motions of the *tang-ki* who is "calculating" what goes on in the world. (This is considered an indication of the god's omniscience.)

Wu Chieh finally extricated herself from this session, but returned in a few minutes and led Mrs. Tan, still gesturing and talking oddly, into her bedroom and got her to lie down. Wu Chieh then fled, but Mrs. Tan did not forget her. She called for her attendance several times over the next few days. Unlike Mrs. Tan, who had spent ten years in the village and was still an outsider, Wu Chieh in the year she had lived in the village had become everyone's confidante, everyone's friend, even Mrs. Tan's.

I have included this long quote from our fieldnotes to give the reader a sense of Mrs. Tan's performances to compare with the description of the session of an experienced *tang-ki* quoted below, and also to provide a glimpse of the way some of the villagers responded to this event. Village opinion was divided at best. Before Mrs. Tan was finally taken away "for a rest" by her mother, several village women reported smelling "puffs of fragrant air" in her room, a sure sign that a god was present; several others reported that she had told them things that only a god could know about their family affairs; she had tormented the Lim family, who had treated her so harshly over the quarrel between their children; she had been visited by a doctor who gave her heavy doses of tranquilizers; and she had held many sessions not unlike the one described above. Finally, old Ong Hue-lieng, who was considered the expert in the region on matters of religion and ritual, came to talk with her. Their conversation, of which we never got a complete report, was not a happy one. He left in a huff.

We began to detect a change in village attitudes shortly after Ong Hue-lieng's visit. Dumb Tien-lai was enjoying the spectacle far too much and talking too openly about how expensive it was for him to have his wife providing free advice to anyone who asked for it. Mrs. Tan spoke too often and too much about herself as Mrs. Tan rather than behaving as a vehicle who was unaware of her pronouncements while "in trance"; her speeches rambled on too long and lost the enigmatic quality that brings authority to the *tang-ki*. And the fact that Ong Hue-lieng was unlikely to recommend that she go to a temple where other *tang-ki* got training and experience seemed to end the matter. Within a week, people had begun to refer to her as "poor Mrs. Tan," to regard her displays as a nuisance, and to pressure members of her family "to do something."

Before I explore in more detail how and why this decision was reached, some background on shamanism, or spirit possession, in China and Taiwan and its role in folk religion is necessary. I will not try to sort out the peculiar amalgam of Buddhism, Taoism, and Confucianism that is involved in folk religion in Taiwan in particular and China in general. Suffice it to say that there are Buddhist temples and monasteries, and their adherents and practitioners are distinguished by dress and diet. There are no Taoist temples, but folk temples devoted to local gods are usually the locus of the activities of Taoist priests and of the lowly spirit mediums (Jordan 1972: 29). The average Taiwanese citizen will make use of Buddhist and Taoist practitioners as the need arises, sometimes entertaining both during funeral rituals. Temples nearly always have at least one Buddhist worthy on their altars, and Buddhist temples sometimes have shrines for local gods in side alcoves. To add to the confusion, spirit mediums in rural areas often provide services from their own home in front of their ancestral altar—which is also a shrine to their particular god—or in the home of the family requesting the help of their god. In urban areas, some *tang-ki* have shop-front shrines to their gods, and the most successful have cults of followers who may themselves perform in trance (Kleinman 1980: 232).

In his study of folk religion in a Taiwanese village, David K. Jordan describes the function of the *tang-ki* at the village level:

The *tang-ki* are the prime rural religious arbiters. It is they who diagnose a given case of familial or village disharmony as caused by ghosts; it is they who explore the family tree or the village forts for possible ghosts and their motivations; it is they who prescribe the cure. Spirit mediums drive harmful ghosts from the village; spirit mediums perform exorcisms; and spirit mediums represent the august presence of the divine at rites performed in their name. It is likely that in the past it was the spirit mediums who had the final voice in alliances between villages [in local wars]. (1972: 85)

But as Jordan goes on to warn:

The *tang-ki* is not a free man, and his imitation of the gods is not a matter of his own caprice. Not only must he perform in trance (and therefore presumably not be guided by capricious desires but only by unconscious directives), but he is subject to charges of being possessed by ghosts rather than by gods should he become incredible. (1972: 85)

And if the *tang-ki* is deemed possessed by a ghost, like any other villager, she will have her soul called back by another practitioner, essentially ending her legitimacy as a shaman.

My own experience with shamans in Taiwan was much more limited than that of Jordan, in part because religion was not the primary focus of my research or that of my co-researcher, Arthur Wolf, and in part because the villages we worked in did not have a resident *tang-ki*. In Peihotien, villagers used the services of an itinerant spirit medium, who visited the area every few weeks, or, late in our stay, of a young man who was attached to a temple in a nearby market town. Neither of these men seemed to have the kind of influence as "religious arbiter" that Jordan describes. Our fieldnotes and the cases the staff recorded of visits to *tang-ki* certainly show that most villagers were "true believers," but we also heard a good deal of the cynicism that Jack Potter (1974) describes when villagers assigned self-serving motives to some of the in-trance pronouncements of local shamans. I do not mean to suggest in any sense that I doubt Jordan's analysis for Bao-an, but only that our informants judged shamans on the basis of their success in solving individual problems—in how *ling* (strong) their gods were. Had I had the foresight to interview more widely, I might have found that spirit mediums had more influence on community matters than I assumed at the time. Considering the case I am discussing here, this would have been an extremely valuable piece of information.

In northern Taiwan, the source of my data and much of the secondary material to which I refer, the village shaman is considered simply a conduit between a god and his petitioners. During festivals celebrating the god, the shaman is expected to put on a display of bodily abuse, such as lying on a bed of nails, or lacerating the body with swords or a prickball. Although this is often called "mortification" in the literature (Jordan 1972: 78), the purpose is not to subjugate the flesh as in early Christian ritual, but to prove that the gods do not allow their vehicles to feel pain from these injuries and will protect their *tang-ki* from permanent damage. The injuries do seem to heal rather quickly, and most observers comment on the absence of any expression of pain. Some shamans draw blood during each session, others only at major public events. In private sessions, they rarely stage such ordeals, but they always trance.

In the literature, there are a number of excellent descriptions of the performances of Chinese shamans. Some focus on the more spectacular (and bloody) feats of *tang-ki* on festival days, when they are showing off the power of their gods (see, for example, Elliott 1955), but a few give us a village perspective. Potter (1974) provides a particularly full picture of what amounts to a village-wide séance in the New Territories in Hong Kong, in which the spirit medium travels through the underworld of spirits, chatting with the departed relatives of fellow villagers and allowing them to convey messages, warnings, threats, and reassurances to the living. A description by Katherine Gould-Martin (1978: 46–47) of a *tang-ki*'s session in a market town not far from Mrs. Tan's home captures the relaxed familiarity of Taiwan shamanism. The god who speaks in Gould-Martin's account is Ong-ia-kong, and a cult has formed around the image of him in the living room of a very devout but otherwise not unusual family. The *tang-ki*, a laborer in his forties who lives two doors away from this family, trances every night after dinner. While petitioners, believers, or just neighbors gather to observe, comment, or seek help, the *tang-ki* wanders about the room, lights a cigarette for the god, exchanges a few words with him, and chats with friends in the crowd. In time, an assistant begins to burn paper money and to chant. As the tempo of the chant increases, the *tang-ki* begins to shake, tremble, and then to jump about, finally banging his head on a table. As Gould-Martin describes it:

Once the *tang-ki*'s head comes down, the assistant stops chanting and begins to read off the first case: "believing man or woman," name, birthdate, address, problem. During the reading the *tang-ki* starts to make sounds in a strange falsetto. He continues for some time. This is considered to be the god speaking in his native dialect, i.e. that which was spoken in his area of the Chinese mainland in the T'ang Dynasty. No one can understand these sounds. The actual advice is given in Taiwanese in a voice similar to the *tang-ki*'s normal speaking voice, but deeper, more forceful, more inflected. The sentences of advice are often followed by, "Do you understand that?" They are interspersed with the falsetto noises. Often there is some discussion. The patient asks the god or the *tang-ki*'s helper a question. The god speaking through the *tang-ki* may reply or, if it is simple or the god seems annoyed, then the helper or even another patient or listener may answer the question. The god does not like to repeat himself and will be annoyed at that, but he will answer further questions. At the end the god, speaking through the *tang-ki*, says, "next case" and lapses into soft falsetto while the data of the next case are read to him. (Gould-Martin 1978: 46)

Once the *tang-ki* has completed the evening's requests to Ong-ia-kong, he is brought out of trance by the assistant's burning of more spirit money, washes his hands and face, chats with whoever is left in the crowd; his evening's work is then over. The money contributed is divided up among the assistant, the *tang-ki*, the host family, and a money box designated for the god's birthday celebration and a temple the group hopes to build in his honor.

The problems brought to *tang-ki* are varied, ranging from illnesses in humans and animals to economic setbacks to marital disputes to fears of infertility. In 1958–59, Arthur Wolf and his field staff collected more than 500 observations of villagers' visits to a local *tang-ki*. Over half the problems brought to the *tang-ki* concerned illness: 53 percent of the women asked about their own or a family member's ill health, and 56 percent of the male visitors sought help for illness. Another 16 percent of the women inquired about domestic discord, and 15 percent of the women inquired about or asked to have their fortune changed. Male clients did not ask as much about family disputes (4 percent) and were more interested in having their fortune tended to (14 percent), seeking help with sick animals (12 percent), and getting advice on financial decisions (8 percent). The following examples from the project's unpublished fieldnotes indicate the kind of information and acuity required of a practicing *tang-ki*.

An old lady asked for advice about her husband, who was seriously ill. The shaman said: "He should have been dead by now. Your husband should have been dead yesterday. However, due to 'strengthened fortune and added longevity' [perhaps from earlier treatment?], he has been able to reach the age of 73. His original life was for only 69 years. Even so, it looks to me like he was supposed to die yesterday. If he survives the first day of the coming month, he will have great fortune. You can then come to me to further strengthen his fortune, but not before." He gave her a *hu-a* [charm paper].

A 17-year-old boy asked about a large protuberance under one of his knees. The shaman said: "You have disturbed some ghosts at night." People in the boy's family admitted that he was often running around outside in the evening and said that the swelling had become larger and more painful in recent days. The shaman gave him a *hu-a* and told him to go see a doctor.

An old lady inquired about her lost gold chain. She said she had come several days before, but after four days of searching, the chain still had not shown up. The shaman said: "Members of your family do not get along with one another and are quarreling. It doesn't matter that you have lost this chain. The quarreling is more important. Take this *hu-a* home and burn it to ashes, mix the ashes in water, and sprinkle it on the roof. You will be in harmony and only then will the chain reappear."

A middle-aged man asked about his chickens. "I have raised some chickens and they seem to have a lot of sickness lately. I don't know whether they have offended some dirty thing or there is some epidemic." The shaman said: "You did not choose a good date when you built the chicken house. Besides, you have offended the fox ghost. Cleanse the chicken house three times with *hu-a* ashes in water. Offer sacrifices to make the fox ghost go away. Then, everything will be all right."

As Kleinman (1980: 218ff) notes, a client's interview with a shaman often takes only a few minutes (although as much as two hours may be spent talking with the assistants and bystanders). In order to address the problems brought before her, a *tang-ki* must have a quick mind as well as a keen understanding of human motivation. Most *tang-ki* recommend medical help for obvious illness and, where appropriate, are also likely to recommend the assistance of other ritual specialists, such as geomancers and herbalists. They also practice a certain amount of psychotherapy (Kleinman 1980). In the examples above, the old woman with the seriously ill husband needed resignation and a bit of hope; the boy clearly needed to see a doctor; a dirty chicken house *might* be causing the man's chickens to get sick; and the old lady who came back because the *tang-ki*'s last bit of advice didn't get her back her gold chain needed distraction—and all families have quarrels.

A successful *tang-ki* must be quick-witted and alert to the needs of her clients ("guest" is the literal translation of the term used). Other researchers (Elliott 1955: 92; Gould-Martin 1978: 59; Kleinman 1980: 217; Potter 1974: 210, 214) have suggested that *tang-ki*'s successes often rest on their knowledge of the social and economic background of their clients.

Kleinman (1980), who interviewed and observed urban *tang-ki* in Taipei, comments extensively on their sensitivity to potential tensions in the Chinese family, even if the particular client/patient did not happen to be known to them.

These "job qualifications" are, obviously, derived from the observation of professional, experienced shamans. My concern in this paper is why Mrs. Tan was eventually considered not *tang-ki* material, why she was never allowed to reach this stage. A number of scholars have discussed the means by which spirit mediums are identified in China, and they report pretty much the same set of expectations (Elliott 1955; Jordan 1972; Kleinman 1980; Potter 1974). *Tang-ki* come from modest socioeconomic backgrounds; they are preferably illiterate; they must be sincere and honest; they must display clear indications that a god has chosen them to be his or her vehicle. People fated to become shamans are originally fated to have short, harmless, unimportant lives, but their lives are extended by the gods who possess them in order that their bodies may be put to good use. Many spirit mediums tell of illnesses in which they were brought back from the dead, after which they were troubled by a god who sent them into trance. Nearly all *tang-ki* in Taiwan report that they struggled against possession as long as they could but finally had to give in to the god's will. In Singapore, according to Elliott, some young men choose the life and train for it, but only after "something happens" to convince them that a god wants to enter them (1955: 163). *Tang-ki*, incidentally, must not charge money for their services, but it is assumed that reasonable gifts will be made by grateful clients. The evidence suggests that in rural Taiwan, few *tang-ki* receive enough in contributions to support themselves without another source of income (Gould-Martin 1978: 62–63; Jordan 1972: 75). As Jordan reports, in rural Taiwan there are few "divine rascals" because the living is too poor (1972: 75).

Anthropologists frequently entertain the theory that spirit possession serves to provide a role for the emotionally disabled, the psychotic, or the epileptic. Kleinman, who studied the *tang-ki* in Taiwan primarily as healers, dismisses this explanation as impossible because of the complex behavior required of shamans:

> Shamanistic healing clearly demands personal strengths and sensi-tivities incompatible with major psychopathology, especially chronic psychosis. Thus my findings argue against the view that shamanism provides a socially legitimated role for individuals suffering from schizophrenia or other severe psychiatric or neurological disorders. (1980: 214)

Kleinman has extensive case material that includes detailed observations of *tang-ki* sessions as well as interviews with both shamans and their clients. His conclusions and those of others who have studied the Taiwan *tang-ki* are in accord with my own observations.

Nonetheless, the behavior of the beginning *tang-ki* and even of experienced *tang-ki* when they are going into trance could well be confused with that of a person who is deranged. (See, for example, the description in Elliott 1955: 63.) And Kleinman himself provides us with a long case study (followed over three years) of a Hakka businessman suffering from acute anxiety and a variety of debilitating physical symptoms, who solved (to his and the shaman's satisfaction) his problems by "accepting the god" of the shrine, trancing, and essentially playing the role of lay shaman in the cult (1980: 333–74). What Western observers might classify as mental illness is not necessarily so classified in Taiwan or China. The Hakka busi-nessman in Taipei was treated for his problems for some time before he was defined as "troubled by the god" who wished to use him as a vehicle. Another of Kleinman's cases, which he classified as "acute, recurrent psychosis associated with normal inter-ictal behavior and provoked by acute stress producing extreme fear," was that of a thirty-four-year-old mother of three who frequently attended *tang-ki* sessions (1980: 166–69). When she began to trance regularly at one of the shrines and "asked that shrine's *tang-ki* if she could become a shaman . . . he told her no (an unusual response), because it was 'too early' and she was 'not yet ready.' " According to Kleinman, the *tang-ki* did so because "the patient was unable to control her trance behavior and acted inappropriately during her trances" (p. 167). The Hakka businessman seemed to have similar difficulties at the outset, but nonetheless was accepted readily as a lay shaman.

Mrs. Tan, our heroine from Peihotien, was eventually deemed "crazy" by her community, or, as Kleinman might more delicately phrase it, to be showing signs of psychopathology. Why? She had as many shamanistic characteristics as others who went on to full *tang-ki* status. Her origins were humble; she was functionally illiterate; she was sincere, devout, and kind-hearted; she had led a harmless and unimportant life; she had a history of psychological breakdown that could be attributed to the god's attempt to make her his vehicle; she had resisted as long as she could; she went into trances and spoke in a voice other than her own. For a fortnight she convinced a fair number of respectable villagers that a god was making his wishes known to them through her. Her lack of finesse in her public performances seemed no more inappropriate than that of other novices described in the literature.* Why, then, did she not qualify as a likely apprentice for training?

Unfortunately, we must depend on anthropological hindsight and the randomly recorded voices of villagers for the answers to these questions. Had Mrs. Tan become a *tang-ki* in Peihotien, we would have pages of fieldnotes on her subsequent career, for having a *tang-ki* in one's village is a source of considerable prestige (Jordan 1972: 81), and certainly

---

*Witness Jordan's description of the initiation of another village woman: "Throngs of village people looked on as she flailed her back, shouting, sputtering, drooling, and muttering. When it was over, she was, willy-nilly, a *tang-ki*" (1972: 167).

something that an anthropologist would want to document, no matter how peripheral ritual behavior might be to her project. But having a near-miss became close to a non-event. We recorded some conversations and asked a few questions, and then quickly turned to other issues. However, even without focused and detailed interviews with Mrs. Tan's neighbors, we can explore some of the reasons why her misery was not validated as divine visitation. From the perspective of her village neighbors, the question was not merely whether she was hallucinating the voice of a god or whether the god was in fact speaking to her. The question included another (for many villagers) more likely alternative: that a malicious ghost rather than a god was tormenting her. When another practitioner diagnosed her illness as a ghost problem, this might have ended the matter, but his treatment appeared to have no effect on Mrs. Tan whatsoever, indicating to her would-be followers that his diagnosis was wrong and the god possession theory was still the best explanation for her behavior.

To understand why Mrs. Tan was not accepted as a vehicle for her god, we must look more closely at her position in her community. A diagnosis of "mental illness" is even less likely to produce a response of care and concern among Chinese villagers than it is among Americans. As long as a family member's oddities can be hidden or explained away, they will be; and whatever the neighbors may think privately, they will go along, for, after all, they, their parents, and their grandparents have lived and worked side by side with this family, sometimes for centuries. Condemning someone with whom your family has that kind of relationship to a status that removes her from participation in society as a fully adult human is not done lightly. One might say that the person's genealogical legitimacy in the community is too high.

In the hierarchy of attributes of legitimacy, Mrs. Tan simply did not rank high enough to protect her from dismissal as a "crazy"; for the same reason, various members of the community who might have recognized her as a potential *tang-ki* decided it was not worth the risk. To begin with, her gender was against her. There are respected women *tang-ki*, but not very many of them. *Tang-ki* are expected to be and do things inappropriate for women, and even though the extraordinary circumstances of a god's demand should make it all right, the sheer incongruity between the expectations of a god's behavior and those of a woman's behavior is enough to create misgivings. *Tang-ki*, even when not in trance and speaking with a god's voice, must be assured and competent individuals. Mrs. Tan's everyday behavior did not inspire this kind of confidence, nor did that of the only known male relative associated with her, Dumb Tien-lai.

Even had Mrs. Tan been male, I suspect her legitimacy would still have received closer scrutiny than that of most men in the village. As noted above, the Tans were "outsiders" in a Lim village. They had no relatives in the area whose genealogy would vouch for their respectability. They were better off than the one or two mainlanders who lived nearby and who were considered totally untrustworthy because they had no family anywhere in Taiwan that could be called to account for whatever transgressions their sons might commit. Nonetheless, the Tans by virtue of their newcomer status remained objects of suspicion and people who were slightly dangerous because they had no family whose face their misbehavior could ruin. The arrival of Mrs. Tan's mother helped, but the presence of her father and his brothers would have helped even more. And here again, her gender was against her, for women are considered only adjunct members of their husbands' families and temporary members of their natal families. There is no solidity, no confidence in ties through females to families about whom one knows nothing.

At another level of abstraction, Mrs. Tan's failure to be judged a *tang-ki*-in-the-making comes down to her ambiguous status in terms of the Chinese concept of the family. Any *tang-ki* treads dangerously near the edge of respectability in relation to Chinese notions of filiality, and Mrs. Tan's situation tipped her into the area of violation. From the view of the Chinese villager, an individual is only part of a more important unit, the family, and the individual's personal inclinations must be subordinated to the needs of that family. Choice of education, occupation, marriage partner, even of medical attention, should be determined by family elders in terms of what is best for the group—and often that group is conceived of as a long line of ancestors stretching into a hazy past and an equally long line of descendants stretching into an unknowable future. The individual is expected to be selfless—even her own body is the property of the ancestors. I have seen innumerable village children harshly punished by their parents for playing so carelessly as to fall and injure themselves, thus damaging the body that belongs to the family. Jordan (1972: 84) also mentions this idea in relation to *tang-ki* who regularly slash, cut, and otherwise mutilate their bodies in service to their god. Although divine intervention is supposed to prevent any permanent damage to the ancestors' property, the *tang-ki* nonetheless violates one tenet of filial piety.

More important, *tang-ki* as *tang-ki* are serving another master. They are expected to be totally selfless in that role as well, submitting themselves fully to the god's will in order to enable the god to solve his followers' problems. In fact, the needs of the ancestors and of the possessing god rarely come into conflict, for when out of trance, *tang-ki* can fulfill all of their obligations to parents, grandparents, and so forth.* However, in theory, *tang-ki* have given their persons to their gods to do with as they will. Thus, *tang-ki* submit to the gods that which belongs to the ancestors. This may make the *tang-ki*'s filial piety suspect, but it also highlights the sacrifice the gods require of their vessels. Mrs. Tan's assumed (though demonstrably inaccurate) rootlessness may very well have served

---

*Gary Seaman (1980: 67) reports that in southern Taiwan novice shamans are ritually adopted by the gods who possess them—literally from their parents. I did not hear of this practice in northern Taiwan.

to devalue the selflessness of her generosity in submitting to the will of the god.

Had Mrs. Tan been the wife or daughter of a Lim, there might actually have been strong pressures on her to accept the nomination of the god whether she wished to or not. In an intriguing study of shamanism in contemporary China, Ann Anagnost describes the pressure put on a woman to assume the role of shaman (1987: 52–54). During a period of failing health, Zhu Guiying exhibited symptoms that were interpreted as spirit-possession. Sought out by fellow villagers as a healer, she at first resisted, but finally submitted to the social expectations of her neighbors. As Anagnost puts it, "To refuse this role would have been tantamount to a denial of social ties and the forms of reciprocity and obligation that bound the community together" (p. 53).

I wish I had been able to pursue Mrs. Tan's case in the years that followed this incident in Peihotien. It is conceivable that in another setting, one where she was known in the context of a family, she might in fact have been encouraged to continue her interactions with the god who approached her in Peihotien. If, for instance, she had moved to Taipei and become involved in some of the cults surrounding well-known urban *tang-ki*, she might have continued to go into trance and might have become a valued member of one of the groups that Kleinman describes, finding peace and status. In Peihotien, she was too low in all of the hierarchies to achieve legitimacy as a full member of her community. As a result, she was not able to overcome her anomaly in either world—that of the village or that of the possessed.

Mrs. Tan did not become a shaman, by one set of measures, because of the structural context in which she lived; she was an outsider—socially and genealogically. But her failure might be accounted for by another set of reasons, reasons even more intimately associated with her gender. Feminist theorists, exploring the construction of the gendered self in white middle-class North Americans, suggest that the male self is based upon a set of oppositional categories (good/bad, right/wrong, nature/culture, etc.) and that male selves are more rigidly bounded, more conscious of a distinction between the self and the other than female selves are (Chodorow 1974; Gilligan 1982, 1988; Hartsock 1983; Martin 1988). A female—perhaps because as Chodorow suggests, the female infant does not need to transfer her identity from her original female caretaker—has a less bounded self. It is not tied into oppositions between self and other, but is constructed instead from connectedness and continuities.* Good *tang-ki* must be able to separate their behavior as *tang-ki* from their everyday behavior. With a self constructed out of dualisms, a male may find it easier to keep his consort with his deity separate from his conscious mental life. Mrs. Tan clearly could not.

In time, Mrs. Tan might have been able to achieve this separation—other female *tang-ki* have. But Mrs. Tan had a special problem. Elsewhere I have explored the construction of the Chinese female self and suggested that it is highly dependent on the meaning given to the individual by others (Wolf 1989). Whereas the Chinese male is born into a social and

---

*I am keenly aware of the dangers of applying theoretical concepts developed from Western data to the analysis of personalities constructed in a very different culture. This hypothesis in particular seems fraught with cultural pitfalls, among them the fact that Chinese children, unlike white middle-class American children, usually have a *variety* of female caretakers during their early childhood. Whether or not the explanations hypothesized by Chodorow, Gilligan, and others have cross-cultural viability remains to be seen, but some aspects of the resulting gender differences they describe in adults appear to translate. See, for example, Martin's (1988: 173ff) description of a female ideology in funeral ritual that emphasizes "the unity of opposites," in contrast to a male ideology that shows "constant efforts to separate opposites," and Rubie Watson's (1986) evidence that personal naming practices in China indicate differences in personhood. Gender differences in personhood and the construction of the self in Chinese society are a seriously neglected topic. Much of the research either asserts there are no differences (e.g., Tu 1985) or ignores gender completely (e.g., Yang 1989) and by default takes the male self to be the Chinese self. I have begun to explore some of these ideas elsewhere (Wolf 1989), and it is a rich area for investigation.

spiritual community that has continuity not only in life but after death, the Chinese female is born into a social community of which she is only a temporary resident, and her spiritual community after death depends upon whom she marries or, more important, whose ancestors she gives birth to. A Chinese boy's self is defined by this certainty, this continuity. A girl's sense of self develops in an environment of uncertainty—if she isn't sufficiently modest, she won't find a good family; if she isn't obedient, no mother-in-law will want her; if she is willful, she will have trouble with some unknown husband. She reads *who* she is in the approving or disapproving faces of those around her. The trauma of Chinese marriage, in which a very young woman is transferred to a distant village where she knows no one, not even her husband, creates for women a crisis of identity that is only resolved by the gradual acquisition of a new set of mirrors in which she can identify herself. Mrs. Tan came to Peihotien a stranger, and a stranger she remained. There was no family to smile or frown, no mother-in-law to approve or disapprove of her behavior, and only a husband who was himself a stranger. Without ties to a family that had an accepted place within the village social system, when Mrs. Tan was no longer a novelty, she ceased to have any identity. She was an outsider who was neither dangerous nor useful, and she was more or less ignored. She was in fact nameless, having lost her personal name at marriage (R. Watson 1986). Unlike other brides, her self was never reconstructed; her mirrors remained cloudy, except for the self she saw reflected in her children and in the conversations she had with the various gods she visited.

I continue to wonder whether or not Mrs. Tan, on that fateful day when she threw herself into the rice paddy, was not, as some claimed, trying to get to the river. Suicide (often by drowning) is a solution for many (younger) Chinese women who have trouble creating a new self in a strange place. Perhaps when she was pulled out of the muck of the paddy, she made one final attempt to join the social world of the village by way of a god who had more reality for her than the people among whom she lived. Unfortunately, her self was so poorly established that she could not carry it off. The self that spoke with the gods could not be used to construct a self capable of surviving in a social world constructed by strangers.

Commentary

Commenting on "The Hot Spell" and on fieldnotes was less problematic than commenting on this essay, in part because the first two texts were created in another lifetime. "The Woman Who Didn't Become a Shaman" is still too close. Instead of using it as it was intended, a third text from the same experience, I find myself searching it for flaws with a parental desire to defend its failings. When I attempted to think about the essay "reflexively," paragraph by paragraph, I felt foolish and quickly became as bored with the project as the average reader was likely to be with the resulting text.

Instead, I have used the essay to look more closely at three areas of concern to both postmodernists and feminists (of all persuasions): audience (readership), authorship, and the selection of research topics. I chose these three both because they happen to interest me and because I seem to find myself consistently marching in the wrong parade whenever I come up against the issues surrounding them. Under audience, I am concerned with whom the ethnographer writes for and what her responsibilities to them consist of. Under authorship, I explore the extent and nature of the authority that accrues when pen is put to paper, and the degree to which it is possible and responsible to share voice/authority/authorship with informants. Under selection of research topics, I sort through some of the postcolonial dilemmas for feminists who wish to continue to set their own research agendas and still behave responsibly toward the people they study.

In their review essay, "Ethnographies as Texts," George Marcus and Dick Cushman identify six readerships of ethnography: the area specialist, the general anthropologist, social scientists other than anthropologists, students, action-oriented readers, and popular readership (1982: 51–52). By and large, their list seems to cover the majority of our readers, but I disagree with some of their statements about why some of the people in their categories read ethnography. For example, the "main critical interest" of general anthropologists is said to lie not so much in the accuracy or clarity of the information presented as "in the craftsmanship of a text, which may offer for emulation a style of argumentation expressed in its handling of realist conventions"(p. 51). Without doing a survey of readers (note Marcus and Cushman's rhetorical assumption of authority here; G. Watson 1987: 35), I would be hard-pressed to prove it, but I am fairly confident that the majority of our colleagues read our work more for its content—be it in search of theoretical or comparative insight—than for its style.

Certainly, feminist anthropologists—those trying to recover women's experience as well as those trying to work out theories of gender asymmetry—are interested in what the ethnographer can tell them of the experience of other women. At the risk of legitimating Clifford's astonishing dismissal of two decades of feminist work ("feminist ethnography has focused either on setting the record straight about women or on revising anthropological categories"; 1986: 21), I hope that feminist anthropologists don't become distracted by postmodernism's preoccupation with form—as so many of our colleagues in the humanities have been—to the neglect of our political agenda, which depends on our discovering all we can about the diversity of women's lived experience. Jane Flax warns:

A problem with thinking about (or only in terms of) texts, signs, or signification is that they tend to take on a life of their own or become the world, as in the claim that nothing exists outside of a text; everything is a comment upon or a displacement of another text, as if the modal human activity is literary criticism (or writing).

Such an approach obscures the projection of its own activity onto the world and denies the existence of the variety of concrete social practices that enter into and are reflected in the constitution of language itself. . . . This lack of attention to concrete social relations (including the distribution of power) results . . . in the obscuring of relations of domination. (1987: 632)

It is here that feminist anthropologists differ from post-modernists like Marcus and Cushman. Our agenda, whether we are engaged in adding to the descriptive material on women's experience or in building theory, is to expose the unequal distribution of power that has subordinated women in most if not all cultures and discover ways of dismantling hierarchies of domination. If our writings are not easily accessible to those who share our goals, we have failed. The dangers of the new forms recommended by postmodernist anthropologists may not be so apparent, but they are no less real for all that. "These new ways of structuring are more subtle and enigmatic than traditional modes of anthropological writing: they may serve to make the new ethnographies more obscure and, thus, difficult for anyone but highly trained specialists to dispute" (Mascia-Lees et al. 1989: 10). Our readership must not be confined to intellectual elites. Given the postcolonial politics espoused by many of the postmodernist writers, I would think they too would be concerned about the limiting factors associated with their experimentation. Who, in fact, *is* their audience?

The intended audience for "The Hot Spell" (although I never tried to publish it) was the general public. Certainly, part of my goal was to spread a little knowledge about the culture in which I was living, but I was far more interested in the characters and their interactions with other beings, embodied and ethereal. The audience for the fieldnotes in Chapter Three was very limited, in the sense that Arthur and I had no intention of distributing them in any way. But they were also written with an audience besides ourselves in mind, one that must be in the consciousness of all neophyte anthropologists who hope they are doing what professionals do. The audience for whom "The Woman Who Didn't Become a Shaman" is intended is clearly anthropological with a feminist leaning, or at least a tolerance for feminism. I was also conscious of the fact that when these events occurred in Taiwan (circa 1960), there were no more than a handful of Taiwanese anthropologists, most of whom studied the material culture of aboriginal groups in the mountains. Now there are many well-trained social/cultural anthropologists, including feminists, studying the Han population. Whether it was this "new" professional audience or the postmodernist rhetoric on ethnographic authority that was responsible, my "findings" are more tentative than they once were, and my conclusions, I hope, more accessible to different interpretations.

Both postmodernists and feminists are concerned about the degree to which ethnographers appropriate the experience of their informants, and some are willing to at least explore the possibilities of co-authorship between ethnographer and informant(s). Clifford says bluntly that plural authorship is still a utopian idea because it is in the end the ethnographer who "assumes an executive, editorial position," and "plural authorship challenges a deep Western identification of any text's order with the intention of a single author" (1988b: 51). Stephen Tyler seems, if anything, to be even less optimistic about polyvocality:

While it is laudable to include the native, his position is not thereby improved, for his words are still only instruments of the ethnographer's will. And if the dialogue is intended to protect the ethnographer's authority by shifting the burden of truth from the ethnographer's words to the native's it is even more reprehensible for no amount of invoking the "other" can establish *him* as the agent of the works and deeds attributed to him in a record of dialogue unless he, too, is free to reinterpret it and flesh it out with caveats, apologies, footnotes, and explanatory detail. . . . These then, are not dialogues, but sophistic texts like those pretenses at dialogue perpetrated by Plato. (As quoted in Marcus & Cushman 1982: 44)

But feminists are accustomed to working toward utopias, and many are willing (at least in theory) to give "the native" freedom to add her own caveats to the text. Some young feminist ethnographers do return copies of their written work to their informants for their approval and encourage them (sometimes to the informant's terror) to put their names on the cover as joint authors. To this feminist, the seriousness of the ethical problems associated with such a plan are surpassed only by the complexity of the practical problems that would arise in attempting to implement it. If one is working in a village at the end of a long trek over land and sea among folk who are not literate in any language, sending back a manuscript would be foolishness or tokenism. Even if the physical conditions are not a serious constraint, the ethics of asking an unsophisticated person or group of people to share in the responsibility of publishing a report on or analysis of their values, attitudes, or even way of life is questionable. Those of us who work in China know that a sudden change in the political climate could make last year's adventure in cross-cultural understanding this year's treason. Under those circumstances, I am willing to bear the label of colonialist, paternalistic foreigner, or whatever, rather than make it necessary for a person who is less aware of the way things work outside her small village to make so dangerous a decision. I think there are a fair number of feminist anthropologists who would share my reticence. Nonetheless, I recognize and respect the political position of those whose commitment to shared authorship causes them to rework and revisit their co-authors until all parties see the manuscript as both safe and fair. Perhaps my misgivings are the result of the politically charged parts of the world in which I have done fieldwork.

There are, of course, other ways of amplifying the voices of one's informants. Assuming at the outset that one is not, as Tyler put it above, "simply shifting the burden of truth," or cleverly marshaling all the voices who support one's interpretation and silencing those who do not, the ethnographer can present the voices of all her informants, including those who disagree. Obviously, this will put her in conflict with her responsibilities to her readers—there are far, far fewer postmodernists with their high tolerance for ambiguity, tedium, contradiction, and ambivalence than there are readers who simply want to find out what the Wiliwili do about adultery. Some Wiliwili may not know, having never encountered such a situation, but when faced by a questioning anthropologist, they will provide a full and complete if nonsensical answer (Keesing 1987: 167–68). And some may know, but when faced by a questioning foreigner, will insist that such a thing never happens in Wiliwililand. But many will both know something about adultery and be willing to tell what they know. Is it not the responsibility of the ethnographer to sort out these voices, saving the nonsense answer for an essay on field methods, the never-happens answer for a chapter on attitudes toward foreigners, and interweaving the partial truths of the others into as complete a story as possible?

The dangers of this realist approach (standard to ethnographers) have been well chewed over by the postmodernists, who generously suggest that we are often not aware of how we use this style to give authority to our creations, concealing even from ourselves alternative explanations or serious cultural rifts. Feminists, speaking from a more openly political position, simply distrust those who are in the more powerful positions. Mascia-Lees et al. state it very well:

From women's position as "other" in a patriarchal culture and from feminists' dialogue and confrontation with diverse groups of women, we have learned to be suspicious of all attempts by members of a dominant group to speak for the oppressed, no matter how eloquently or experimentally. (1989: 33)

To be suspicious is good. To allow it to silence one is something else. Sorting the oppressor from the oppressed has never been easy once we began to recognize the complexities of power that result from differences in race, class, and gender. But I think I would prefer to have my decisions grounded in a feminist politic rather than arising from a rhetorical need to "decenter" the ethnographer and her authority.

Superficially, it seems that "The Woman Who Didn't Become a Shaman" is not polyphonic. Aside from one long quote, the voice is mine or that of other anthropologists. But we are not talking here about literal translations of informants' precise words. I present several explanations of what happened to Mrs. Tan, most of which came in one form or another from villagers. I am not "speaking for them," but I am the one who is presenting those of their opinions—insofar as I understood them—that might make sense to my readership. Am I appropriating the collective experience of people from Peihotien for my own purposes, for my personal career needs? Yes, I suppose this is true.

However, had I not written about Mrs. Tan, no one else would have, and although I don't think it would make a whit of difference to her one way or another, I did not ask her then and I have no way of finding her now. She, like everyone else in Peihotien, was made aware of the reasons we were living there, but I assume, like many of her neighbors, if she thought about our presence at all, she accepted our "studies" as just part of the oddities associated with non-Han barbarians. After a good deal of soul-searching, I decided that the publication of the three texts that center on an event in her life would have more positive results than negative. If nothing else, she and her ordeal have been given a good deal more dignity than her neighbors were willing to offer. And we have learned a bit more about the effect of patriarchal thinking on aberrant behavior, the way in which different kinds of power is expressed in a village setting, and perhaps even something about representations in texts. I am, I fear, too irretrievably attached to Enlightenment projects to rid myself of the conviction that there is something emancipatory in knowledge.

Which brings me to my third topic in this Commentary, deciding what to become knowledgeable about. Choosing a research topic sounds rather like a chapter title in an elementary methodology textbook, but it could also be one in a book of feminist ethics. One of the corollaries of feminist anthropology is that if feminists believe they should work toward the liberation of all women, then their research should be focused on projects that benefit women. At the same time, feminist social scientists are concerned that their research not exploit women and have searched for more equitable ways of carrying out field research. Some feminists attempt true collaboration with their informants, asking them to select the research problem, help collect the data, and participate in the analysis of those data. The assumption is that kinship studies are of no interest to women whose children are dying of malnutrition. This is a hard position to argue against, even when the choices are not so stark. But it is also a hard proposition to implement on a practical level. I have tried to imagine how I might have involved the women in my various research sites in designing a project that would both benefit them and interest them. The thought is numbing. I suspect the only truly successful projects of this sort would involve some kind of economic development. The locally designed projects I have read about were either of particular interest to a small group of women or, frankly, not worth the incredible investment of time and energy expended by both researchers and researched. The end result was to be praised more for the process than the product.*

Acquiring basic knowledge about human behavior sounds like a very male-directed project, but our basic knowledge about gender is still limited and confusing. What we have

---

* An exception is Elizabeth Enslin's study (1990). The Nepalese village women she worked with first wanted to become literate and then, because of the difficulties in finding a safe classroom in which to study, wanted a women's center. They defined Enslin's research project in terms of their own needs.

learned thus far may point us in the right direction, but I would hate to be suddenly given the power to transform society on the basis of our current understanding of gender. Some of our postmodernist critics dismiss such thoughts and suggest that if even the possibility of a truthful representation of another culture is hopeless, "knowledge" is not of much practical value. But there are many feminist anthropologists who would disagree. As Sandra Harding points out:

Feminists in the scientific traditions have attempted to reform and transform the theories and practices of these traditions in order to create less partial and less distorted representations of the world than the mainstream androcentric ones. They want less false stories about nature and social life; they want scientific explanations that can provide useful guides to improving the conditions of women. (1990: 83)

In this postcolonialist period, we need to be sensitive to the sins of our fathers (and not a few of our mothers), but we also need to be aware of the different needs of the many feminisms. In some countries, feminist researchers do not have the luxury of contemplating the larger picture, or, for that matter, the luxury of tolerating the goals of white middle-class feminists from U.S.-European culture. That does not mean that we should set our goals aside in order to implement theirs. If we have the means to assist them, fine, but we should not abandon our own intellectual goals out of some misguided desire for political correctness. Quoting again from Harding:

The postmodernist critics of feminist science . . . appear to assume that if one gives up the goal of telling one true story about reality, one must also give up trying to tell less false stories. They assume a symmetry between truth and falsity. Yet, even Thomas Kuhn argues that it would be better to understand the history of science in terms of increasing distance from falsity rather than closeness to truth. . . . Feminist inquiry can aim to produce less partial and perverse representations without having to assert the absolute, complete, universal, or eternal adequacy of these representations. (1990: 100)

There may be no absolute, complete, universal or eternal truth, and thus far feminist anthropologists have undermined an impressive number of formerly true stories. It is essential that we continue wherever and however we can to revise the old truths, but it is also essential that we begin to construct new, less false stories.

CHAPTER FIVE

Writing Ethnography: The Poetics and Politics of Culture

THE TITLE OF this chapter is, obviously, a play on the title of Clifford and Marcus's celebrated collection of essays, *Writing Culture: The Poetics and Politics of Ethnography* (1986). I use it not out of disrespect for that important set of papers, but because it captures how different my perspective on ethnography is from that of Clifford and Marcus. We are not in the business of anthropology, as Clifford Geertz so nicely states it, "to capture primitive facts in faraway places and carry them home like a mask," but rather "to reduce the puzzlement," to discover "the informal logic of actual life" (1973: 16–17). Some of us hope to uncover the cross-cultural commonalties that underlie our diversity; more of us hope only to reduce the puzzlement about one or two unfamiliar places.

The means by which we acquire the experience that starts us on the path to understanding—our field methods—have always been eclectic and, as a result, slightly troubling to our colleagues and to us. We do not sit around in our villages and atolls absorbing culture like sunshine, as some of our postmodernist critics appear to think. In fact, most of us exhaust ourselves mentally and physically in our attempts to see, hear, and experience as much as we can in the too brief period academic schedules allow for fieldwork. We *do* research. It is not something that simply happens to us as a result of being in an exotic place. Our willingness to speak and write about that experience results from our serious engagement in discovering what we can about how life is lived in another social/cultural setting.

The first field trip is a stunning roller coaster of self-doubt, boredom, excitement, disorientation, uncertainty, exhaustion, bullying, being bullied, cajoling, being cajoled—in the course of which we somehow accumulate "data," precious notebooks packed with disorganized thoughts, detailed observations of minutiae, descriptions of rituals, transcripts of conversations, diagrams, and detritus. Doing fieldwork is a matter of being in the right place at the right time (not necessarily the time your informants told you would be the right time) and asking the right questions of a wide variety of people. Unfortunately, we rarely know the right place, right time, right question, or right people until we have nearly finished the job, or *have* finished it and are three thousand miles away. We are dependent upon our ability to match up clues, our luck in following hunches, a couple of chance encounters, an observation jotted down that only makes sense days or even years later. Some of us do systematic and well-organized interviews and observations in the field, but in the end, when the stack of filled notebooks is much higher than the stack of blank and waiting notebooks, when we ask ourselves if we have the material to "reduce the puzzlement," we as often as not have no answer and leave the field site because we must, not because we feel we have finished the work.*

The experience of fieldwork does not produce a mysterious empowerment, but without it, the ethnographer would not encounter the context—the smells, sounds, sights, emotional tensions, feel—of the culture she will attempt to evoke in a

---

*Indeed, as Mac Marshall pointed out to me, one *never* finishes the job, because each time we return to the field, the people we study have changed, and each new insight brings new questions. If we ever did fully remove the puzzlement, either the culture would have disappeared from the face of the earth or we would be wrong.

written text. Before I lived in Taiwan, I had seen beautiful *National Geographic* pictures of rice paddies inhabited by water buffalo and peasants in quaint hats. This did not prepare me for the intense stench of "night soil" (human feces mixed with water and allowed to stew in the sun for a few weeks before being poured into the flooded paddy) or for the despair with which an unemployed middle-school graduate turns over the putrid muck of his father's land. There was nothing mystical or even pleasant about most of these experiences, but without them, my ability to convey any part of their meaning would have been seriously compromised.

Experience is messy. Searching for patterns in behavior, a consistency in attitudes, the meaning of a casual conversation, is what anthropologists do, and they are nearly always dependent on a ragtag collection of facts and fantasies of an often small sample of a population from a fragment of historical time. When human behavior is the data, a tolerance for ambiguity, multiplicity, contradiction, and instability is essential. When we at last sit down at a clean desk in a quiet study and begin to assemble the vivid images and cryptic notes, searching for a coherency, we must constantly remind ourselves that life *is* "unstable, complex, and disorderly" (Flax 1987:643), everywhere. As ethnographers, our job is not simply to pass on the disorderly complexity of culture, but also to try to hypothesize about apparent consistencies, to lay out our best guesses, without hiding the contradictions and the instability.

How in heaven's name do we do that? As Clifford asks for us:

If ethnography produces cultural interpretations through intense research experiences, how is unruly experience transformed into an authoritative written account? How, precisely, is a garrulous, overdetermined cross-cultural encounter shot through with power relations and personal cross-purposes circumscribed as an adequate version of a more or less discrete "other world" composed by an individual author? (1988b: 25)

Clifford in particular, and the postmodernists in general, not only object to the way anthropologists have attempted to answer these questions in the past, but question the ethnographic enterprise itself—our ability to understand what we see if we are not of that culture, and the ethics of presenting such understandings as fact. They assert that the self of the ethnographer should be decentered in terms of the authority of voice, but at the same time should be front and center in the text so that the reader is constantly aware of how biased, incomplete, and selective are the materials being presented.

And yet, as Clifford himself points out, if the ethnographer can construct culture in her writings, she can also construct a self, an example of which can be found in the short story in Chapter Two, which was written long before I knew anything about reflexivity and at a time when "modern" was still being "with it." Clifford assumes in "On Ethnographic Self-Fashioning: Conrad and Malinowski" (1988d: 97) that the "real" Malinowski is not the Malinowski of the *Argonauts* but the one of the *Diary*. I don't see one self as any more real than the other: they simply show different aspects of Malinowski's personality. Moreover, their literary construction occurred at different times. The ethnographic self I am constructing here is very different from the one I created in "The Hot Spell" or for that matter in my 1968 book, *The House of Lim*. Which of these constructions is my "real" self?

How, then, is a fully reflexive experimental ethnography going to be an improvement over "realist" accounts, where the rules are at least fairly well known? In a sense, Clifford comments on this himself when he says:

Thus the discipline of fieldwork-based anthropology, in constituting its authority, constructs and reconstructs coherent cultural others and interpreting selves. If this ethnographic self-fashioning presupposes lies of omission and of rhetoric, it also makes possible the telling of powerful truths. But . . . the truths of cultural descriptions are meaningful to specific interpretive communities in limiting historical circumstances. (1988d: 112)

The "telling of powerful truths" is possible but perhaps confined to specific communities that share the rules? Surely this kind of known authoritative voice is safer than the artifice of the fictionizer, who has no obligations beyond making the text plausible, interesting, and faithful to whatever aesthetic integrity is peculiar to the period's genre?

Renato Rosaldo, in a book that is wonderfully accessible and gently reflexive, warns: "If classic ethnography's vice was the slippage from the ideal of detachment to actual indifference, that of present-day reflexivity is the tendency for the self-absorbed Self to lose sight altogether of the culturally different Other" (1989: 7). Although Rosaldo agrees with those who have declared a crisis in the production of ethnography (p. 38), he is not content with solutions that mystify the ethnographic process further, such as leaving the work of making sense of the text to the reader. Rosaldo explains:

Alien cultures, however, can appear so exotic to outsiders that everyday life seems to be floating in a bizarre primitive mentality. Social descriptions about cultures distant from both the writer and the reader require a relative emphasis on familiarization, so they will appear—as they also in fact are—sharply distinct in their differences, yet recognizably human in their resemblances. (1989: 39–40)

Rosaldo also points out that the reverse is true when the culture being subjected to analysis is one's own. "Social descriptions by, of, and for members of a particular culture require a relative emphasis on defamiliarization, so that they will appear—as in fact they are—humanly made, and not given in nature" (p. 39).

"Defamiliarization" is not a term feminists have used, but ever since second-wave feminism empowered feminist social scientists in the late 1960s, we have employed the technique. In order to make gender a proper subject of study, we first had to locate women in culture and society, and then get our colleagues to recognize that their location is no more natural than that of the male half of humanity. As Pat Caplan indicates, the latter task has been absurdly difficult: in England, research on women—whether done by feminists or not—has been dismissed as just another specialization, ignoring the feminist critique that addresses issues of *gender* and should concern the discipline as a whole (Caplan 1988: 14). In the United States, the opposition for a long time came from those who viewed our openly revisionist agenda as merely political, therefore not objective scholarship, hence discountable. Now that the postmodernists have themselves problematized the concept of objectivity, feminists might expect serious attention to the work they have already done on the very issue that was formerly used to condemn them (Harding 1990). Reflexivity, it seems, does not begin at home: postmodernists who criticize social science with a terminology that requires learning a new vocabulary seem unable (unwilling?) to "read" the feminist work unless feminists who speak postmodernism make the translation for them.*

Before reflexivity was a trendy term, feminists were examining "process" in our dealings with one another—questioning the use of power and powerlessness to manipulate interactions in meetings, examining closely the politics of seemingly apolitical situations, evaluating the responsibilities we bore toward one another, and so on. The awareness developed in these small "consciousness-raising" sessions quickly spilled over into the work world of social scientists who recognized their double responsibility as feminists doing research on women. I do not mean to imply that *all* feminist social scientists are reflexive in their research and writing, but it is much more common to find a serious questioning of

---

*The essays by Deborah Gordon (1988) and Frances Mascia-Lees et al. (1989) speak directly to the writing of ethnography. A broader spectrum of the feminist translators can be found in Linda Nicholson's excellent new collection, *Feminism/Postmodernism* (1990).

methodology and creative involvement of both researched and researchers among feminists than in the work of mainstream social science (e.g., Haraway 1985; Harding 1987; Shostak 1981; Stacey 1988).

Whether we are talking about nonexploitative methodology in field research or authority in writing ethnography, we are talking about power—who has it, how it is used, for what purposes. This is what the study of gender, class, and race is really about: how subordinated sectors accommodate to and resist the power of privileged sectors, how privilege (like resistance) is camouflaged, how power is earned, learned, and occasionally spurned. Just as the reality of male privilege affects the lives of every woman, whether she is conscious of it or not, the concept of power is by definition a factor in every feminist's research. Feminist standpoint theorists claim that those who occupy a subordinate position will have a more complete and less distorted knowledge of the system under which they live, and that only through struggle against the oppressing group can a researcher acquire knowledge of the social reality she wishes to study (Harding 1987; Hartsock 1983; Nash 1976). This is a very appealing theory, intellectually and politically, but it creates problems for feminists who do not work in their own society. (Marilyn Strathern points out some of these problems, but at the same time she makes the error of assuming that *all* feminist anthropologists are standpoint theorists—which we are not.) According to standpoint theory, it would be almost impossible for me to understand the oppression of Chinese women or to understand my own potential for being an oppressor in a postcolonial research project.

When the Western anthropologist first strolls into a thirdworld village, she is a walking symbol of her native country's power, assuming (as is usually the case) that she is white and accompanied by boxes bristling with modern technology. If the anthropologist is male, his panoply of power is further enhanced. After the first pratfall, the anthropologist's aura of power may be tempered, but it is still taken seriously. Within a few months, specific situations become factors in the influence of the still obvious differential power relations. In a Chinese village, the anthropologist, if she is to be one, learns quickly to be deferential to people older than herself, to males, and to those who have taken on the role of teacher. She does not lose the power associated with being a "guest" from a rich and powerful country, but as she tries to negotiate her way through the complexities of village life, her observers become more aware of her dependency on them and less conscious of her power over them.

In our concern over our colonial luggage, we tend to forget the complex power negotiations that also go on among individuals. Even the most arrogant neocolonialist soon discovers that one cannot order rural people to reveal important thoughts about their culture. For at least the first few months, most fieldworkers are dependent on their informants to help them figure out what the questions are (and in some environments, how to stay alive). Those who carry the culture and those who desperately want to understand it may participate in a minuet of unspoken negotiations that totally reverses the apparent balance of power. An extreme example of this is E. E. Evans-Pritchard, who strode into Nuerland with the confidence of his race and education—and was led around by the nose by the unwilling subjects of his study (1969). Wu Chieh, our field assistant in Taiwan, was all too conscious of our privilege as Americans, but the longer she was in our employ, the more power she had over the success of our project—a fact she was quite aware of and on occasion put to good use.

The inequalities of power that exist when first-world anthropologists work in third-world countries must be recognized as playing a major role in our research results, but they are not the only factors, and they may in some circumstances be higher in the consciousness of the anthropologists than in the informant's. For example, when Margaret Rodman became seriously ill while doing fieldwork with her husband on the island of Ambae, it soon became clear that heroic measures would be required if her life was to be saved. The headman of the village, who was their host, prime informant, and good friend, made one set of plans, and her husband made another, conflicting set. Both men were shocked and profoundly surprised when the other did not, in this serious emergency, automatically submit to his obvious authority (Rodman & Rodman 1990). In this case, and in other examples each of us could draw from our own fieldwork, the locus of power/authority is not so obvious as it might seem from the distance of the first world. In our desire to avoid objectifying our informants, we run the risk of patronizing them.

The feminist's sensitivity to power as a factor in all our research, and our enhanced understanding (through political struggle) of both the ubiquity of gender asymmetry and the deep roots of male privilege, should make us even more cautious about postmodernist "reforms" than other social scientists. The male-dominated traditions of the sciences, social sciences, and the humanities have been the accepted reservoirs of knowledge (and the source of power) for centuries, and their guardians can now afford to modestly reconsider the partialness of their truths and the ambiguities in the construction of their knowing.* Feminist work has always been under suspicion, often for the same things the postmodernists' critiques now celebrate—like questioning objectivity, rejecting detachment, and accepting contradictory readings. Feminists who have only recently gained some academic security might think carefully about whether intense reflexivity in their research and writing will be evaluated as being in the new postmodernist mode or as simply tentative and self-doubting. Feminists would also do well to consider whether following a postmodern Pied Piper might not lead them away from a

---

*For an intelligent summary of these positions, see Linda Nicholson's Introduction to *Feminism/Postmodernism* (1990: 1–16), and for a more thorough exploration, see the other essays in the collection.

commitment to the research and struggle that is hard because it is feminist. How many women, feminist or not, are defining the issues around the postmodernist seminar tables?*

Anthropologists always have searched and, I trust, always will search for ways to improve their research and make the results of that research more accessible to their various audiences. James Clifford, George Marcus, et al., as part of the postmodernist fascination with style and rhetoric, suggest that we are in crisis (Clifford 1988a; Clifford & Marcus 1986; Marcus & Fischer 1986) because we have claimed an authority that does not exist, told truths that are only partial, and (mis)represented an Other that conceals the construction of the Other by an invisible anthropological Self. Their solutions to these problems, however, do not include better ways of doing fieldwork, but different (better?) ways of writing ethnographies. Paul Roth suggests of the postmodernists, "Authority is taken to accrue not, as before, from the role of field scientist but rather from that of author" (1989: 555). Indeed, any authority the field scientist attempts to assert as a result of her research can be held against her.

Nonetheless, the postmodernist critique has encouraged a lot more reflection (reflexivity?) in recent years about ethnography as both process and product than many of us recognize. If we are not all becoming more reflexive, some of us are at least becoming more self-conscious.† Anthropology has a politics and has always had a politics, one aim of which is to help Western society recognize itself as but one community among many human communities (Mascia-Lees et al. 1989: 8). Al-

---

*Steven Sangren (1988) raises some of these same issues, although not necessarily as a caution to feminists.

†This may, alas, be similar to the "affirmative action" rhetoric of university administrators who insist on having a woman and a person of color on every committee, preferably chairing it, without troubling to change their ideology one whit. It is simply another bureaucratic requirement to be met or explained away. The "reason" for the requirement is irrelevant.

though of different theoretical persuasions, most anthropologists would probably accept that basic goal if translated into their particular vocabulary. But this period of intensified reflexivity has made a good many of us take stock of who is now in our audience and of how ragged the line between our community and the communities we study has become.

To my thinking, if there is any crisis in ethnography, it is a growing uncertainty about our dual responsibility to our audiences and our informants. If there is a conflict, which should be privileged? At first glance, that seems obvious—of course, we must protect our informants above all else. Those are the ethics of our profession. But how far does this go? Judith Stacey found herself forced "to collude with the homophobic silencing of lesbian experience" because she had agreed to give her informants a pre-publication veto over a manuscript (1988: 24). Others have found themselves in similar politically compromised situations. And some of us have found ourselves making paternalistic decisions to avoid potential harm to informants. More and more often now our informants are also of the community for whom we write. Then what? And what of conflicting interests among our informants? These are not new problems, but they have become more complex problems because we can no longer assume that our analyses will not be read by our informants (or their enemies). We can no longer assume that an isolated village will not within an amazingly short period of time move into the circuit of rapid social and economic change. A barefoot village kid who used to trail along after you *will* one day show up on your doorstep with an Oxford degree and your book in hand.

The growing presence of third-world scholars among our readership and in the discipline itself certainly increases the pressure on us to think carefully about what we publish, and it also gives us another kind of understanding of the societies we study. We have all recognized at one time or another in our research that each field experience allows us to peel back yet one more layer of meaning—those who were raised in the culture have more immediate access. However, as those who have done research in their own culture are aware, there are also disadvantages to studying "at home." To do it success- fully requires a great deal of reflexivity, and that may be even more difficult for third-world anthropologists competing in first-world academia, where there are those who doubt their competence because they *are* third-world and those who re- sent their competence for the same reason. Openly discussing one's problems with rapport in the field or one's bouts of irritability during fieldwork or similar reflections might be good methodology to one group and good ammunition to another whose members do not wish one well.

The blurring line between readers and informants carries one set of responsibilities, but there is a new set of responsi- bilities to our audiences that seems to have eluded the post- modernist critics, although I am not the first to mention it (e.g., Caplan 1988; Mascia-Lees et al. 1989; Sangren 1988). Experimental ethnography so obscure that native speakers of English with a Ph.D. in anthropology find it difficult to un- derstand is written for a small elite made up primarily of first- world academics with literary inclinations. The message of exclusion that attaches to some of these texts contradicts the ostensible purpose of experimental ethnography, to find bet- ter ways of conveying some aspect of the experiences of an- other community. The message to nonacademics who simply want to know what the foreigner has to say about them is confusing at best.

So what will come of all this? Some of our colleagues will not notice that "an experimental moment in the human sci- ences" (Marcus & Fischer 1986) has come and gone; others have already dismissed it; some of us will find ourselves more self-conscious about what we do in the field and how we write about what we did when we return home; some of us will not be aware of how much we have changed until some fearless graduate student draws it to our attention in a term paper; some of us will gradually drift off into writing fiction. I suspect that in no time at all the alarming banners of a new generation of crusaders for prefuturist studies will unfurl, provoking outrage among the old postmodernist graybeards.

References Cited

References Cited

Anagnost, Ann S. 1987. Politics and Magic in Contemporary China. *Modern China* 13(1): 40–61.

Bodman, Nicholas C. 1955. *Spoken Amoy Hokkien*. Kuala Lumpur: Grenier and Sons.

Bordo, Susan. 1990. Feminism, Postmodernism, and Gender-Scepticism. In Linda J. Nicholson, ed., *Feminism/Postmodernism*, pp. 133–56. New York: Routledge.

Caplan, Pat. 1988/1989. Engendering Knowledge: The Politics of Ethnography. *Anthropology Today* 4(5): 8–12; 4(6): 14–17.

Carrithers, Michael. 1988. The Anthropologist as Author: Geertz's *Works and Lives*. *Anthropology Today* 4(4): 19–22.

———. 1990. Commentary on Paul A. Roth, "Ethnography Without Tears." *Current Anthropology* 31(1): 53–55.

Chodorow, Nancy. 1974. Family Structure and Feminine Personality. In Michelle Z. Rosaldo and Louise Lamphere, eds., *Woman, Culture, and Society*, pp. 43–66. Stanford, Calif.: Stanford University Press.

Clifford, James. 1986. Introduction: Partial Truths. In James Clifford and George E. Marcus, eds., *Writing Culture: The Poetics and Politics of Ethnography*, pp. 1–26. Berkeley: University of California Press.

———. 1988a. *The Predicament of Culture: Twentieth-Century Ethnography, Literature, and Art*. Cambridge, Mass.: Harvard University Press.

———. 1988b. On Ethnographic Authority. In *The Predicament of Culture* (1988a), pp. 21–54.

———. 1988c. Power and Dialogue in Ethnography: Marcel Griaule's Initiation. In *The Predicament of Culture* (1988a), pp. 55–91.

————. 1988d. On Ethnographic Self-Fashioning: Conrad and Malinowski. In *The Predicament of Culture* (1988a), pp. 92–113.

Clifford, James, and George E. Marcus, eds. 1986. *Writing Culture: The
Poetics and Politics of Ethnography*. Berkeley: University of California Press.

Crapanzano, Vincent. 1980. *Tuhami: Portrait of a Moroccan*. Chicago:
University of Chicago Press.

Dumont, Jean-Paul. 1978. *The Headman and I*. Austin: University of
Texas Press.

Dwyer, Kevin. 1982. *Moroccan Dialogues*. Baltimore: Johns Hopkins
University Press.

Elliott, Alan J. A. 1955. *Chinese Spirit Medium Cults in Singapore*.
Monographs on Social Anthropology, no. 14: London School of Eco-
nomics and Political Science.

Enslin, Elizabeth. 1990. The Dynamics of Gender, Class, and Caste in
a Women's Movement in Rural Nepal. Ph.D. dissertation, Stanford
University.

Evans-Pritchard, E. E. 1969. *The Nuer*. Oxford: Oxford University
Press.

Flax, Jane. 1987. Postmodernism and Gender Relations in Feminist
Theory. *Signs* 12(4): 621–43.

Geertz, Clifford. 1973. Thick Description: Toward an Interpretive
Theory of Culture. In *The Interpretation of Cultures*. New York:
Basic Books.

Gilligan, Carol. 1982. *In a Different Voice: Psychological Theory
and Women's Development*. Cambridge, Mass.: Harvard University
Press.

————. 1988. Adolescent Development Reconsidered. In C. Gilligan, J.
V. Ward, and J. M. Taylor, eds., *Mapping the Moral Domain*, pp. vii-
xxxviii. Cambridge, Mass.: Harvard University Press.

Gordon, Deborah. 1988. Writing Culture, Writing Feminism: The Poetics and Politics of Experimental Ethnography. *Inscriptions* 3/4: 7–24.

Gould-Martin, Katherine. 1978. Ong-Ia-Kong: The Plague God as
Modern Physician. In Arthur Kleinman, Peter Kunstadter, E. Russell
Alexander, and James L. Gale, eds., *Culture and Healing in Asian
Societies: Anthropological, Psychiatric and Public Health Studies*,
pp. 41–67. Boston: G. K. Hall.

Haraway, Donna. 1985. A Manifesto for Cyborgs: Science, Technology,
and Socialist Feminism in the 1980s. *Socialist Review* 15(80):
65–107.

Harding, Sandra. 1990. Feminism, Science, and the Anti-Enlightenment

Critiques. In Linda J. Nicholson, ed., *Feminism/Postmodernism*, pp. 83–106. New York: Routledge.

———, ed. 1987. *Feminism and Methodology*. Bloomington: Indiana University Press.

Hartsock, Nancy. 1983. *Money, Sex, and Power: Toward a Feminist Historical Materialism*. Boston: Northeastern University Press.

Jackson, Jean E. 1990. "I am a Fieldnote": Fieldnotes as a Symbol of Professional Identity. In Roger Sanjek, ed., *Fieldnotes: The Makings of Anthropology*, pp. 3–33. Ithaca, N.Y.: Cornell University Press.

Jordan, David K. 1972. *Gods, Ghosts, and Ancestors: The Folk Religion of a Taiwanese Village*. Berkeley: University of California Press.

Keesing, Roger M. 1987. Anthropology as Interpretive Quest. *Current Anthropology* 28(2): 161–76.

Kleinman, Arthur. 1980. *Patients and Healers in the Context of Culture: An Exploration of the Borderland Between Anthropology, Medicine, and Psychiatry*. Berkeley: University of California Press.

Lederman, Rena. 1990. Pretexts for Ethnography: On Reading and Fieldnotes. In Roger Sanjek, ed., *Fieldnotes: The Makings of Anthropology*, pp. 71–91. Ithaca, N.Y.: Cornell University Press.

Lutkehaus, Nancy. 1990. Refractions of Reality: On the Use of Other Ethnographers' Fieldnotes. In Roger Sanjek, ed., *Fieldnotes: The Makings of Anthropology*, pp. 303–23. Ithaca, N.Y.: Cornell University Press.

Malinowski, Bronislaw. 1922. *Argonauts of the Western Pacific*. London: Routledge.

———. 1967. *A Diary in the Strict Sense of the Term*. New York: Harcourt, Brace, and World.

Marcus, George E. 1986. Afterword: Ethnographic Writing and Anthropological Careers. In James Clifford and George E. Marcus, eds., *Writing Culture: The Politics and Poetics of Ethnography*, pp. 262–66. Berkeley: University of California Press.

Marcus, George E., and Dick Cushman. 1982. Ethnographies as Texts. *Annual Review of Anthropology* 11: 25–69.

Marcus, George E., and Michael M. J. Fischer. 1986. *Anthropology as Cultural Critique: An Experimental Moment in the Human Sciences*. Chicago: University of Chicago Press.

Marshall, Mac. 1989. Rashomon in Reverse: Ethnographic Agreement in Truk. In Mac Marshall and John L. Caughey, eds., *Culture, Kin, and Cognition in Oceania: Essays in Honor of Ward H. Goodenough*, pp. 95–106. Washington, D.C.: American Anthropological Association Special Publication no. 25.

Martin, Emily. 1988. Gender and Ideological Differences in Representations of Life and Death. In James L. Watson and Evelyn S. Rawski, eds., *Death Ritual in Late Imperial and Modern China*, pp. 164–79. Berkeley: University of California Press.

Mascia-Lees, Frances E., Patricia Sharpe, and Colleen Ballerino Cohen. 1989. The Postmodernist Turn in Anthropology: Cautions from a Feminist Perspective. *Signs* 15 (11): 7–33.

Mohanty, Chandra Talpade. 1984. Under Western Eyes: Feminist Scholarship and Colonial Discourses. *Boundary* 12(3)–13(1): 333–58.

Nash, June. 1976. A Critique of Social Science in Latin America. In June Nash and Helen Safa, eds., *Sex and Class in Latin America*, pp. 1–24. New York: J. F. Bergin.

Nicholson, Linda J., ed. 1990. *Feminism/Postmodernism*. New York: Routledge.

Obeyesekere, Gananath. 1981. *Medusa's Hair*. Berkeley: University of California Press.

Okely, Judith. 1975. The Self and Scientism. *Journal of the Anthropological Society of Oxford* 6(3).

Ottenberg, Simon. 1990. Thirty Years of Fieldnotes: Changing Relationships to the Text. In Roger Sanjek, ed., *Fieldnotes: The Makings of Anthropology*, pp. 139–60. Ithaca, N.Y.: Cornell University Press.

Plath, David W. 1990. Fieldnotes, Filed Notes, and the Conferring of Note. In Roger Sanjek, ed., *Fieldnotes: The Makings of Anthropology*, pp. 371–84. Ithaca, N.Y.: Cornell University Press.

Potter, Jack M. 1974. Cantonese Shamanism. In A. P. Wolf, ed., *Religion and Ritual in Chinese Society*, pp. 207–31. Stanford, Calif.: Stanford University Press.

Probyn, Elspeth. 1990. Travels in the Postmodern: Making Sense of the Local. In Linda J. Nicholson, ed., *Feminism/Postmodernism*, pp. 176–89. New York: Routledge.

Rabinow, Paul. 1977. *Reflections on Fieldwork in Morocco*. Berkeley: University of California Press.

———. 1986. Representations Are Social Facts: Modernization and Postmodernity in Anthropology. In James Clifford and George E. Marcus, eds., *Writing Culture: The Poetics and Politics of Ethnography*, pp. 234–61. Berkeley: University of California Press.

Rodman, William L., and Margaret C. Rodman. 1990. To Die on Ambae: On the Possibility of Doing Fieldwork Forever. In Philip R. DeVita, ed., *The Humbled Anthropologist: Tales from the Pacific*, pp. 101–20. Belmont, Calif.: Wadsworth Publishing Company.

Rosaldo, Renato. 1980. *Ilongot Headhunting, 1883–1974: A Study in Society and History.* Stanford, Calif.: Stanford University Press.

———. 1989. *Culture and Truth: The Remaking of Social Analysis.* Boston: Beacon Press.

Roth, Paul A. 1989. Ethnography Without Tears. *Current Anthropology* 30(5): 555–69.

Said, Edward. 1978. *Orientalism.* New York: Pantheon.

Sangren, P. Steven. 1988. Rhetoric and the Authority of Ethnography: "Postmodernism" and the Social Reproduction of Texts. *Current Anthropology* 29(3): 405–35.

Sanjek, Roger, ed. 1990. *Fieldnotes: The Makings of Anthropology.* Ithaca, N.Y.: Cornell University Press.

Schieffelin, Edward. 1976. *The Sorrow of the Lonely and the Burning of the Dancers.* New York: St. Martin's Press.

Seaman, Gary. 1980. In the Presence of Authority: Hierarchical Roles in Chinese Spirit Medium Cults. In Arthur Kleinman and T. Y. Lin, eds., *Normal and Abnormal Behavior in Chinese Culture,* pp. 61–74. Boston: D. Reidel.

Shostak, Marjorie. 1981. *Nisa: The Life and Words of a !Kung Woman.* Cambridge, Mass.: Harvard University Press.

Smith, Robert J. 1990. Hearing Voices, Joining the Chorus: Appropriating Someone Else's Fieldnotes. In Roger Sanjek, ed., *Fieldnotes: The Makings of Anthropology,* pp. 356–70. Ithaca, N.Y.: Cornell University Press.

Smith, Robert J., and Ella Lury Wiswell. 1982. *The Women of Suye Mura.* Chicago: University of Chicago Press.

Stacey, Judith. 1988. Can There Be a Feminist Ethnography? *Women's Studies International Forum* 11(1): 21–27.

Strathern, Marilyn. 1987. An Awkward Relationship: The Case of Feminism and Anthropology. *Signs* 12(2): 276–92.

Tu, Wei-ming. 1985. *Confucian Thought: Selfhood as Creative Transformation.* Albany: State University of New York Press.

Tyler, S. A. 1982. Words for Deeds and the Doctrine of the Secret World: Testimony to a Chance Encounter Somewhere in the Indian Jungle. *Proceedings of the Chicago Linguistics Society,* quoted in Marcus and Cushman 1982 above.

Van Maanen, John. 1988. *Tales of the Field: On Writing Ethnography.* Chicago: University of Chicago Press.

Watson, Graham. 1987. Make Me Reflexive—But Not Yet: Strategies for Managing Essential Reflexivity in Ethnographic Discourse. *Journal of Anthropological Research* 43: 29–41.

Watson, Rubie S. 1986. The Named and the Nameless: Gender and Person in Chinese Society. *American Ethnologist* 13(4): 619–31.

Wolf, Margery. 1968. *The House of Lim: A Study of a Chinese Farm Family.* New York: Prentice-Hall.

———. 1989. The Self of Others, the Others of Self: Gender in Chinese Society. Paper presented at a conference on Perceptions of the Self: China, Japan, India. East-West Center, University of Hawaii, Aug. 1989.

———. 1990a. The Woman Who Didn't Become a Shaman. *American Ethnologist* 17(3): 419–30.

———. 1990b. Chinanotes: Engendering Anthropology. In Roger Sanjek, ed., *Fieldnotes: The Makings of Anthropology*, pp. 343–55. Ithaca, N.Y.: Cornell University Press.

Yang, Mayfair Mei-hui. 1989. The Gift Economy and State Power in China. *Comparative Studies in Society and History* 31(1): 25–54.

Index

Index

In this index an "f" after a number indicates a separate reference on the next page, and an "ff" indicates separate references on the next two pages. A continuous discussion over two or more pages is indicated by a span of page numbers, e.g., "pp. 57–58." *Passim* is used for a cluster of references in close but not continuous sequence.

Library of Congress Cataloging-in-Publication Data

Wolf, Margery.
  A thrice-told tale : feminism, postmodernism, and ethnographic responsi-
bility / Margery Wolf.
    p. cm.
  Includes bibliographical references and index.
  ISBN 0-8047-1979-9 (cloth : acid-free paper)
  ISBN 0-8047-1980-2 (pbk. : acid-free paper)
  1. Ethnology—Methodology. 2. Ethnology—Philosophy. 3. Feminist
criticism. 4. Postmodernism—Social aspects. 5. Anthropology—Taiwan—
Field work. 6. Taiwan—Social life and customs. I. Title.
GN345.W65 1992
301—dc20   91-24593

  ♾ This book is printed on acid-free paper

Original printing 1992

Edwards Brothers Malloy
Ann Arbor MI. USA
November 12, 2015